ROCKY SPIRIT

ROCKY SPIRIT

The Rocky Balboa Connection to Success

Felice Cantatore

iUniverse, Inc.
Bloomington

Rocky Spirit
The Rocky Balboa Connection to Success

Copyright © 2012 Felice Cantatore

All rights reserved. No part of this book may be used or reproduced by any means, graphic, electronic, or mechanical, including photocopying, recording, taping or by any information storage retrieval system without the written permission of the publisher except in the case of brief quotations embodied in critical articles and reviews.

iUniverse books may be ordered through booksellers or by contacting:

iUniverse
1663 Liberty Drive
Bloomington, IN 47403
www.iuniverse.com
1-800-Authors (1-800-288-4677)

Because of the dynamic nature of the Internet, any Web addresses or links contained in this book may have changed since publication and may no longer be valid. The views expressed in this work are solely those of the author and do not necessarily reflect the views of the publisher, and the publisher hereby disclaims any responsibility for them.

Any people depicted in stock imagery provided by Thinkstock are models, and such images are being used for illustrative purposes only.

Certain stock imagery © Thinkstock.

ISBN: 978-1-4697-0727-3 (sc)
ISBN: 978-1-4697-0726-6 (hc)
ISBN: 978-1-4697-0725-9 (e)

Library of Congress Control Number: 2012900549

Printed in the United States of America

iUniverse rev. date: 2/24/2012

Dedication

God
*It is with deepest gratitude that I accept the mission to share Your message.
Thank You for the blessing of this journey.*

My Parents
Mary & Angelo
*Mom and Dad, you gave me life, heart and soul.
Your love and guidance has allowed me to achieve success.
From you, I learned to be a loving husband and father.
I will always appreciate and love you.*

For my wife
Chrissy
and our daughters
Gina Marie and Adriana
*Thank you for your continuous love and support.
You inspire me every moment of every day.
I love and adore you.*

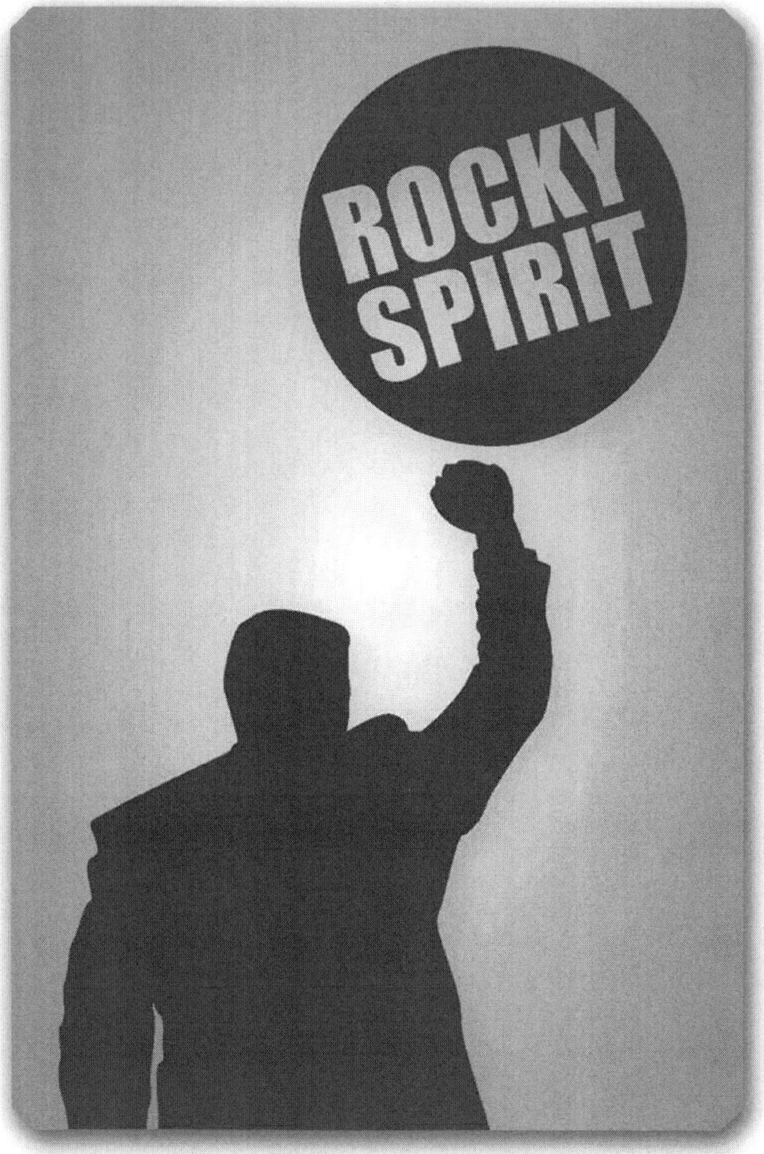
ROCKY
SPIRIT

Acknowledgments

Gratitude: The state of being grateful; warm and friendly feeling toward a benefactor; kindness awakened by a favor received; thankfulness

It is with sincere gratitude that I express appreciation to all who have influenced my life's journey. This book is proof that anything is possible with the support of family and friends.

To my brothers and sisters, Maria Cantatore, Nicholas Cantatore, Doreen Polizzi, Salvatore Cantatore and Angela Dougherty, thank you for your guidance through the years that allowed me to learn and grow from your experiences. I am forever grateful to be your brother. We will always walk together through every challenge and success.

To the rest of my family and friends, you are all a part of the spirit of the journey. Thank you for your continuous love, support and inspiration through the years.

I would like to bestow special thanks and gratitude to Marcy Neumann, President of Heartlites Incorporated, LLC. *Rocky Spirit* would not have been possible without your affirmation, interest and contribution. Your words, *"think again,"* were the motivating force to complete my journey. Thank you, thank you, thank you for every piece of advice and everything that you taught me. To the memory of your son, Jacob Neumann: May his everlasting spirit shine through as we make a positive impact on the world.

The *Long Island Press* and its owners Ron Morey and Jed Morey for your consistent support, encouragement and for embracing me like family. To Jed: Thank you for completely understanding the journey and your contributions to this book. Dan Chozahinoff and Harlan Friedman, you both once worked by my side and have remained wonderful friends. Your kinship is strongly felt in this story. To all of my co-workers who have supported me, especially Christopher Twarowski, for your editing assistance and masterful word craftsmanship, David Wexler for photography, Sal Calvi for graphic design and Beverly Fortune for being the final eyes before going on press.

To Coach Ray Bettinelli of Bettinelli's Community Boxing Academy, your words gave me clarity and your coaching gave me strength. Your work teaching the great sport of boxing and your dedication to children will be your legacy. You became a mentor and a great friend.

Jimmy Gambina: Your boxing, life and spiritual wisdom taught me many lessons. Your work in the original Rocky is incredible. It is my hope that others who watch your performance in the ring during the boxing scenes see what I see: a man who is totally dedicated to his trade and goodness in the world. Thank you for your advice, prayers, and blessings. I trust we will always be friends, in your words "exactly."

Mark O'Laughlin, thank you for being a gracious opponent. There are good people in this world and you are one of them. May God bless you and your family.

Lori Ames, The PRFreelancer, Inc., thank you for your insight into the publishing industry and for making yourself available when I needed advice. Your son Robert motivated me with his positive spirit and outlook on life.

No book is complete without great editing and I had the pleasure of working with two of the best. To Carol Hoenig and Linda Rae Roggensack: Thank you both for helping my voice and message become a reality.

Contributing thanks to the following people: Peter Iannucci, Joe Bacarella, Robert Resnikoff, Karen Garvey, Donna Martini, Frank Scarpa, Tom Piccininni, George Nedeff from iUniverse, all of my associates and every person mentioned in this book.

In Memorium

In special memory of James LiCastra,
"Uncle Jimmy"
for being a special part of my childhood
and a terrific person to our family.

In loving memory of my Father,
Angelo Cantatore
for being my guiding spirit.

Extreme gratitude to my sister,
Doreen
Her Rocky Spirit carried me over the finish line.
This book was made possible by her motivation
and desire to go the distance.
We did it!

Produced by
Rocky Spirit Productions LLC

www.rockyspirit.org
felice@rockyspirit.org
rockybalboa1@aol.com

Contents

INTRODUCTION
Opening Bell
1

ROUND ONE
Sign from Above
3

ROUND TWO
Childhood Connections
7

ROUND THREE
Living the Rocky Life
11

ROUND FOUR
Attracting a Goal
19

ROUND FIVE
Measure of a Man
29

ROUND SIX
Is it the Law of Attraction?
37

ROUND SEVEN
Manifesting the Opportunity
45

ROUND EIGHT
Ringside in Las Vegas
57

ROUND NINE
Next Steps
73

ROUND TEN
The Plan
87

ROUND ELEVEN
Golden Ticket
111

ROUND TWELVE
Defining an Orb
121

ROUND THIRTEEN
Confirming a Universal Law
127

ROUND FOURTEEN
Training Montage
143

ROUND FIFTEEN
Fight Night
161

THE EPILOGUE
Final Bell
173

INTRODUCTION

Opening Bell

Success: The achievement of something desired, planned or attempted.

Have you ever wondered who or what guides us through life? *Rocky Spirit* is a fifteen-round true story that will resonate with any individual inspired to believe that they can accomplish anything. It will convey that things happen for a reason, and for every action there is a reaction that contributes to the movie script of our lives.

This is a story about an everyman who followed a childhood passion toward a series of goals that define the meaning of personal success. It begins with the revelation of a circle of energy and spiritual sign from a photograph related to a glorious experience involving a franchise of inspirational boxing movies and its main character.

The photograph became the motivation to recall every interesting detail, starting from childhood, which would connect me to these iconic films. They eventually led to the pursuit of a life-fulfilling quest to also go the distance no matter the outcome. Like an old-time boxer, I symbolically trained for a vision. Through the years, I enhanced my so-called footwork and thought process. I learned how to take and deliver a punch while being influenced by multiple lessons from a collection of six motion pictures about an underdog fighter.

There are many interesting connections linking my life to these films. They include a number of chance meetings with the actors, the highs and lows of a mission to appear as a movie extra, an ingenious effort to score a golden ticket to attend the premiere of the last sequel and much more.

I will share the details about the first time I met the series creator, Sylvester Stallone and his alter ego in person. The experience sparked my creativity to write a newspaper cover story titled, "On the Set of *Rocky Balboa*," which earned a first-place journalism award for Best Arts Story from the Press Club of Long Island.

This timeless journey about heart, perseverance and goal-setting will bring clarity to a phenomenon known as the Law of Attraction and Spiritual Energy. Its purpose is to become a roadmap for others to help manifest their own personal success utilizing their passions to either achieve or overcome what is present in their physical world. Your thoughts become reality and guide you to discover your inner Rocky Spirit.

An objective of this book is to motivate readers to pursue their dreams and recognize that a champion resides in your heart. Every cast member from the original film would agree that the movie captured the true American spirit in its purest form. As love poured out from each one of them, they shared the understanding that there is a little Rocky in all of us.

My name is Felice Cantatore, an Italian born in the City of New York, a media executive living a simple life in the suburbs. I am a large man, standing six foot, one inch tall and weighing well over two hundred pounds, a super heavyweight in the sport of boxing, but just a plain man in the sport of life.

I am the youngest in a family of six children born to parents who lived the American Dream after overcoming personal challenges in their youth. Due to circumstances beyond their control, my parents both lacked a connection to their fathers and struggled against the odds but came together to persevere and succeed. Their values would continually influence me and help build my character to become a competitor.

This story takes the reader on a journey where I end up, like Rocky, in the ring as an underdog boxer for a charity event. The final step of this astonishing experience becomes a powerful purpose to define the meaning of the word success. It will shed light on the circle of influence that surrounds our universe and has guided my life. The message would be revealed through a unique connection to the spirit of Hollywood and a movie character named Rocky Balboa.

ROUND ONE

Sign from Above

City of Philadelphia, Pennsylvania
The Philadelphia Museum of Art
December 18, 2006

Standing in the middle of the Philadelphia Museum of Art, I was breathing in every sensation. It was one of the most satisfying nights of my life. My wife Chrissy and I had been guests at the 2006 exclusive reception—the afterparty following the gala premiere of the film *Rocky Balboa*. It was official. My appearance onscreen as an extra, sitting ringside during the big fight scene had made the final cut. Ever since I saw the original movie back in the late Seventies, it had been a dream to become part of the *Rocky* universe.

I was overwhelmed with gratitude for having accomplished this seemingly impossible goal. As the exhilarating event wound down, the cast and most of the guests were long gone. Only a handful of us remained on the once-crowded main floor as the waitstaff began their cleanup duties. Another round in my lifelong *Rocky* journey was about to end, but this was a night I would remember forever. *Could it ever be better than this?*

As I looked around the room one last time, my eyes were drawn to an extraordinary art exhibit. A gold crucifix that seemed to be bursting with energy caught my attention. I began to mentally recap the night's events while many thoughts flowed through my mind. My own personal *Rocky* story up until this night was one similar to what Sylvester Stallone had created, one that I had grown up admiring since I was eleven years old. I had been just another so-called bum from the neighborhood, so how did I do it? How did I become a part of this amazing event along with actually appearing in the movie?

Energy from the franchise of *Rocky* films paralleled my life and became a timeline throughout the decades. Few other films have impacted so many people around the world. This one motivated me to achieve another planned goal, which is what brought us to the premiere in Philadelphia.

On this night, in this iconic location, I shared the vibration of energy with like-minded people. It was the only place in the universe I wanted to be at this moment. Standing in the middle of the Great Stair Hall, I recalled every detail of the evening's events and my lifelong association with *Rocky*. I thought about the challenge of going the distance and what might happen next.

Noticing my contemplative mood, Chrissy turned to me with her pretty smile and in a soft, tired voice asked, "Are you done?"

I knew what she was hinting at. She really meant, not only was I done for the night, but was I done chasing this crazy, so-called *Rocky* Dream?

It had been thirty years of what some people might call fanaticism, but Chrissy understood and endorsed my passion for what I regarded as the *Rocky* Phenomenon. I nodded yes, I was done.

I took her hand, and together we walked out the front doors of the museum. We crossed the expansive stone terrace and headed toward the top of the famous Rocky Steps that overlooked the city of Philadelphia. My deep desire to be a part of this movie was now complete.

I stopped at the top of the steps and looked out at the illuminated skyline. It was a clear, crisp, almost magical, December evening, just past the stroke of midnight. I looked at Chrissy and said, "Just one more thing."

"What now?"

"Could you take one more picture?"

We were standing in the very spot where the Rocky character had stood in the original film. A bronze plaque with an imprint of two Converse Chuck Taylor sneakers commemorates the exact location. I wanted Chrissy to take a final photograph of me striking a victory pose, with one arm raised high in the air like the *Rocky Balboa* movie poster. This everlasting memory would symbolize my journey, with all the emotion, vibrating energy and fervor that empowered me to become part of the *Rocky* legacy.

Chrissy was probably hoping to finally get off her feet after a long night of socializing, but she agreed to take the picture. She stepped back to get a full image as I looked out at the city with my back to the camera and my large frame looming before its lens. I raised my fisted arm toward the midnight sky.

"Are you ready?" she asked.

"Go for it."

I heard the shutter click. At the same time, Chrissy experienced a loud popping noise, coupled with an unexpected flash of brilliant, white light. The surprise impact jolted her small body a step backward.

"Whoa!" she shouted.

I spun around to ask what happened. She looked puzzled and said, "It broke. The camera broke."

"What do mean the camera broke? That's impossible. I've been using it all night. Take another one."

Chrissy was sure the bizarre flash on the screen of her digital camera had rendered it inoperable. She had owned it for quite awhile and had never experienced anything like it before. I asked her again to take another photo and resumed my pose. This time it worked as if there never had been a problem.

"That was so weird," she said. "I never saw anything like that before. It was a huge flash of white light."

We laughed over the mysterious incident as we descended the steps to head back to our hotel. As we strolled down the street hand in hand, the Philadelphia Museum of Art and its famous entrance faded into the background. We shared a hug while hailing a cab. What I thought would be the end of my story would actually become the beginning of a new journey.

It wasn't until we were home the next night when I downloaded the photos and the large flash of light proved to be an epiphany. What happened next did transform my life, all because of this unexplainable photograph and my newfound knowledge of a spiritual connection.

All of us probably have a moment in time when we recognize a monumental change in our life's direction. I thought my purpose in standing on those steps at that exact moment was to celebrate the end of a great run of luck that had gotten me to a place where I wanted so much to be. I didn't realize then that it would turn out to be a new beginning. So what was so extraordinary about the flash of light and its astonishing effect? As I continue to share the timelines of this story and the relationship between a six-part series of *Rocky* films, it will clarify its meaning.

The answers go back to 1977, when I was an unwitting eleven year-old boy and the Law of Attraction began to manifest in my life. This universal principle holds that you attract what you think about: Your thoughts bring physical results into reality. This concept connected me to *Rocky,* a motion picture that fascinated me and captured the spirit of a young boy that has continued throughout my adult life.

I remember every detail of how this American classic became important to me, including the very first time I ever heard of it. The original film was spiritually unique and way ahead of its time. As people are receptive to its sacred connections, my story's message will become a rebirth of the Rocky Spirit to the world of today for tomorrow's sake.

The entire series of movies explore a human spirit that comes from the heart. This story will share the value of a motion picture experience from the 1970s and the sequels that followed, which continue to provide positive influences into the life of an everyman.

ROUND TWO

Childhood Connections

It was winter in early 1977, and it seemed like any other day in the life of an eleven year-old boy. I had just finished helping my brother with his daily newspaper delivery. Dressed in an old, grayish-green snorkel coat, maroon Sears Toughskins jeans and scuffed, supermarket, generic-brand sneakers, I pedaled to Gardner's Luncheonette on the main boulevard to buy a chocolate bar.

Gardner's, a traditional mom-and-pop shop, was the best candy source in the neighborhood. It featured a soda fountain counter with round, black-cushioned, spinning seats. Some had little rips in them, but they were comfortable and fun to sit on. Toward the back of the store there were greeting cards, small gifts and other items, such as school supplies. In the front of the store stood a comic book, magazine and newspaper stand, and opposite that, a candy counter. A large vintage cash register sat high up on a platform.

Arthur and Helen Gardner were the proprietors of this landmark sweetshop. I was a frequent visitor because my brother Sal hired me to help him fold and deliver the original version of the old *Long Island Press*. How could I know that the namesake of this publication would someday be an important part of my life? At the time, my brother was a savvy entrepreneur. He figured he could pay me two dollars a week while he collected and pocketed twenty to thirty dollars a week for himself. That was big money for a kid back in the Seventies. He must have learned his skills from the original master paperboy in the family, our oldest brother Nick, who probably broke him into the business in a similar manner. For me, however, it certainly felt like a fair deal as it gave me the expendable income to purchase some candy or bubblegum cards.

On this occasion, it didn't take me long to grab a Milky Way bar and proceed to the register to pay. Waiting in line, I was seconds away from an introduction to a movie called *Rocky*.

Mrs. Gardner, a sweet woman with short, curly grey hair and a pleasant smile, was chatting with an older gentleman in front of me. They were discussing what she called one of the greatest movies she had ever seen. Mrs. Gardner had to be in her mid sixties, so I figured she must have watched a lot of classic films in her time. I listened in on the conversation as she vividly described to the customer the excitement that this movie had generated.

Their dialogue caught the attention of Mr. Gardner, a tall, senior fellow, burly but friendly. He always wore a white, food-stained apron and could talk your ears off about any topic. Once he started speaking, you couldn't escape him. Mr. Gardner also shared his enthusiasm about what he had witnessed on the big screen. "In all my years, I have never seen anything like it," he remarked.

I still remember the excitement on his face when he described how people jumped up and down in the theater and cheered throughout the movie, especially at the end. Each time Mr. Gardner said something to the customer, he glanced over to include me in the conversation. After the gentleman paid for his newspaper and left the store, Mrs. Gardner turned to me and said, "Have you seen the movie?"

"No, ma'am."

"Well, you better see it, young man," Mr. Gardner chimed in. "You won't be sorry!"

They again went into detail how the theater audience erupted in excitement over this film. They continued on for several minutes, repeating how everyone reacted to this underdog boxer and his heroic saga. I was captivated and wanted to see the movie that night. Finally, I saw an opening to pay for my candy bar and escape their never-ending review. I thanked them and left the store, but not without promising to see this movie called *Rocky*.

That was all I thought about while pedaling my bicycle home. Once there, I grabbed the newspaper and opened it to the entertainment section. I found an ad that proclaimed *Rocky* was up for a few Academy Awards, including Best Picture. It listed all the theaters where it was playing, and I saw one that was familiar to me.

"Cool!" I said out loud to myself. "It's at the UA Quartet."

That was our neighborhood theater right down the road from our home. I noted the times it was playing and immediately thought about the one person who would almost never say no if I asked him to take me to the movies. That person would be Sal, the richest paperboy I ever met. He was nearly sixteen and had already been driving the family car, a green, 1973 Oldsmobile Cutlass Supreme, for some time. My brother agreed to take me to see what the woman in the candy store claimed to be one of the greatest movies she had ever seen.

Hours later, my brother, his girlfriend Liz and I were off to the theater for the 7:35 p.m. show. Sal was always very generous and usually paid for everything. As he was buying the tickets, I studied the *Rocky* poster in the display case. It was the same one I'd seen in the newspaper advertising that the movie was up for several Academy Awards. That poster and pose seared a lasting memory in my mind. I stood there staring at it with the image of Rocky standing on top of some steps with his arms raised in victory.

"Let's go, I got the tickets," my brother said.

The three of us entered the theater, each with a large buttered popcorn and soda in hand. We walked toward the black-and-white doors with a number 2 on the front of them and fell in at the end of the line, next to the burgundy velvet ropes. *Rocky* was still being featured in two of the four theaters, months after its release. Once inside, we rushed in to find good seats. The room was filling up quickly. We secured three toward the front on the left-hand side and settled in. Minutes later, the house lights lowered and we were ready to view a film that was about to become a consistent part of my life.

ROUND THREE

Living the Rocky Life

My first memory of the movie was, of course, the inspirational sound of the theme song as giant letters spelling out R-O-C-K-Y scrolled right to left across the screen. It was so simple, and yet so memorable; I still smile every time I see it.

In the first scene, creator Sylvester Stallone and director John G. Avildsen show an image of Jesus Christ as the camera pans down to the ring. Rocky Balboa is fighting a guy named Spider Rico in an old church that was converted into a dingy boxing arena in Philadelphia. The invocation of Jesus suggests that everyone needs God in their corner. The image seemed to symbolize a parallel between the actor's personal faith in the Lord and that of the Rocky character. That faith was depicted throughout the entire run of the franchise. The intention of the scene was to convey Rocky as the Chosen One.

A minute or two into the film, as I bonded with its main character, he was unfairly butted in the head by his opponent. In a rage, Rocky pummeled him to the floor and left the ring, holding a towel to his bloody forehead. The ringside crowd hurled paper cups and other objects, calling him a bum, but he was oblivious to their jeers. The movie hooked me in right then and there. Rocky is then seen in the locker room putting on his robe. On the back of it was his nickname, "The Italian Stallion." This moniker would later help change his life and eventually set him on a path toward reaching his goal and personal success to go the distance.

Before you know it, Rocky is talking to his pet turtles, Cuff and Link, and his goldfish, Moby Dick. By then, I was rooting for this tough guy in the leather coat and black hat who was always shrugging his shoulders, shadow boxing and bouncing a black rubber ball. After witnessing his rage in the ring, I began to see his soft side through his love for animals. He even showed compassion as an intimidating money collector for a neighborhood loan shark when he chose not to break the thumb of a deadbeat borrower.

One by one, I was introduced to the supporting cast: Adrian, Mick, Paulie and Apollo Creed. Each character was uniquely flawed and I could easily relate to them. I was intrigued by Rocky's girlfriend, Adrian, played by actress Talia Shire. She is shy, and I fell in love with her later on when the once-ugly duckling is transformed into a vibrant beauty in her bright red hat and coat. Adrian was a character you could sympathize with, and I began to root for her as well.

I respected the gym manager, Mick, played by the legendary Burgess Meredith, maybe because I knew him as the Penguin, the famous villain in the *Batman* television series. I appreciated Mick's wisdom in the film and later learned that many of his lines were ad-libbed. I was furious at him when he made Mike, the gym attendant (played by Jimmy Gambina, a real-life boxing trainer), bag up Rocky's gear from his locker and leave it on skid row. Eventually, though, like Rocky, I forgave him and gained admiration for this man of experience.

Next we were introduced to Rocky's faithful-but-crazy friend Paulie, played by actor Burt Young. I put up with his antics because I knew Rocky cared about him. Paulie, Adrian's brother, had a solid relationship with the Southpaw from Philly.

Apollo Creed, the perfectly sculpted World Heavyweight Champion, was played by the athletic actor Carl Weathers. He reminded me of the charismatic boxing legend Muhammad Ali, and it was hard not to like him. Creed selected the Italian Stallion as his next opponent from a book of fighters because of that nickname. Rocky, a no-name fighter, got a million-to-one shot to become "A Somebody."

Lastly, there was Philadelphia. This blue-collar city played a key role as the ideal setting for the story. The music and the training scenes tied it all together. The movie was filled with character and characters. It was a recipe of many ingredients that, when mixed together, produced a feast.

I watched every scene of this film as intently as any young eleven year-old possibly could. The beef-punching and training montage were exciting, and who could forget the raw eggs? Even though I didn't, I wonder how many kids imitated that egg-drinking scene. I was spellbound throughout the entire movie, but it was the big fight that really knocked me out. The ending of the film was the beginning of the franchise and marked the start of my own parallel story.

Rocky's only goal was to go the distance; to still be standing in the fifteenth round at the final bell. No fighter had ever gone fifteen rounds with Apollo Creed. In an important scene before the fight, Rocky confided to Adrian that if he could just go the distance, he would know for the first time in his life that he was not "just another bum from the neighborhood." His sentiment became a metaphor for the film and a mantra that I would use throughout my life to also have the desire to succeed.

I read that the powerful scene was almost cut out of the movie because of budget and time constraints and that Stallone was adamant to include it. The actors were given only one take to get it right and, like magic, it came out perfect. Burt Young believed that this "magic" is what made the film so special.

I was nervous and tense when it came time for the fight scene. My stomach was churning and my knees were knocking like I was the one heading into that ring. I looked over at my brother and he was all in. I could tell he was already thinking about rushing home to drink some raw eggs and plan his own training montage to the *Rocky* theme song. So began the search for our inner Rocky.

As the fight commenced, every single person in the theater was on their feet, cheering and yelling at the screen, urging Rocky to go the distance. It was just like the Gardners said it would be. There was total mayhem in the theater, and I've never seen anything like it before or since.

My heart raced until the very end, when it started pounding right before the final bell. Could the Southpaw from Philly pull off a miracle? Creed's back was against the ropes, and Rocky was landing some lethal blows to the champ's chin. The crowd in front of me screamed as they jumped up and down. The people behind me were climbing on the backs of our seats. Then the timekeeper (played by Stallone's actual father, Frank Sr.) started ringing the bell: ding, ding, ding. That sound was the last thing I heard as the audience erupted.

It was sheer chaos in the ring and in the theater. Everyone was shouting, clapping and talking so loud that I completely missed one of the great lines in the movie when Rocky asked Adrian, "Where's your hat?" as she entered the ring after the decision. Rocky had just fought the toughest battle of his life, but was so locked into his love for this girl that he was concerned about the smallest detail, her hat. It was a clever metaphor about their relationship.

I struggled to hear over all the commotion who had won the fight. I never heard the ring announcer give the results, but my eyes were focused on the screen. When Apollo Creed raised his hands in victory, I knew I had witnessed one of the most dramatic endings in movie history.

I was disappointed and excited at the same time; all of my young emotions were attacking my inner spirit. The screen froze on the embrace of Rocky and Adrian, and all I could think about was that he did it, he went the distance. That one second would last forever and define their life together. It was a pinnacle moment and their perfect ending as both experienced true love and personal success.

That one second became meaningful in so many ways. As I watched the embrace, I recognized that this man faced one of his greatest physical challenges, not only in the boxing ring, but in his life. His quest was to become "A Somebody," to prove that his life's purpose was fulfilled. The heart and desire to go the distance that Stallone portrayed in Rocky's character earned him the respect of the supporting cast and millions of viewers around the world.

At the moment of the embrace, the actor/writer became that somebody of his desired intention. That inspirational tableau transcends time. The same sentiment has been attributed to Stallone in real life. The public perception is that the producers tried to purchase the script and cast a more famous actor to play the lead role, but Stallone stubbornly refused because he wanted to be Rocky Balboa himself. In one of many clever moves, the people behind the scenes made Stallone become Rocky and Rocky become Stallone.

As the credits started to roll, I knew that America's new-found hero had gone the distance and his life now had meaning. It wasn't just the fight, but the love from a girl and their against-the-odds relationship that was important. No one told me it was a love story, but to an eleven year-old boy, it didn't really matter.

The entire audience watched every credit and stayed by their seats until the screen went dark. The excitement level remained high even as we left the theater. The pure energy of that movie was incredible. We spilled out onto the sidewalk, raving about the masterpiece we had just witnessed. The three of us were emotionally exhausted, but physically energized. My brother and I shadow-boxed while humming the theme song "Gonna Fly Now" in front of the theater. And we weren't the only ones dancing around; hordes of moviegoers pretended to be Rocky. We knew we had just experienced something special.

The next day, I could hardly wait to go to the candy store to thank Mr. and Mrs. Gardner. That movie review is their legacy. As I look back, they touched my life that day, and I will always have gratitude toward them.

Days, weeks and months after seeing the blockbuster for the very first time, it was all I would talk about. *Rocky* mania was running rampant. It seemed like everyone in the neighborhood had seen the movie except for one of my close friends, Peter, who lived up the block. Like the Gardners did for me, I urged him to see it as soon as he could so we could share in the triumph of the excitement.

The original *Rocky* is still the greatest in-theater experience ever, even after all these years. The sign of a great movie is when it leaves you wanting more. We wanted Rocky to win that big fight, but either way, he was still our new-found hero. I went back to the theater and saw it over and over again. In those days, you would pay to see a favorite film multiple times. I remember waiting forever for *Rocky* to hit commercial television. Back then there were no VCR or DVD players. Sometimes, I would try to catch a glimpse of the movie on television through squiggly lines on something called WHT Channel 68, one of the first subscription pay channels.

About a month or two after we'd seen the movie numerous times, the annual Academy Awards show was ready to air. In the Seventies, whenever television played clips from a movie still in the theaters, it was a big occasion because we didn't have video options back then. I had never cared much about the Oscars before, but this time I had to root for the Italian Stallion and my favorite motion picture. I counted the days to that show, wondering if *we* would win.

If I was nervous watching the fight scene in the movie, I was really jumpy the night of the Academy Awards. Stallone, with his newfound stardom similar to his Rocky character, was sporting a tuxedo with an open shirt and no tie. It was an unusual look for a formal affair, but we were told during the program that he had busted his bow tie while getting ready, so he decided to go without it. It really looked like he was an underdog.

My Dad and I watched the show together that night. I'm not even sure if he had seen the movie, but he got a kick out of me squirming throughout the program. It is one of those childhood memories of my Dad that I really enjoy. The whole night was a race between *Rocky* and a monster of a movie called *Network* for Best Picture. It was also Stallone against some guy named Peter Finch for Best Actor. I learned that night that Finch unfortunately passed away before the Academy Awards show, making him the sentimental favorite to win.

The suspense was intense as I waited for the announcement and it was stressful for a little guy. Everyone said *Network* was pretty good, but because of the competition it gave my favorite movie that night, it turned me away forever.

Finally it was time for the Best Actor award. As actress Liv Ullman announced the nominees, I was lying on the floor in front of the family television set. I assumed the position of any kid growing up in the Seventies: on my stomach with a pillow from the couch stuffed under my chest, my hands flat on both sides of my face propping up my head. Finally, I couldn't take the suspense anymore, and I rolled over. I didn't even look at the television as Ms. Ullman, speaking in her Norwegian accent, said the words, "And the winner for Best Actor is—Peter Finch for *Network*."

I rolled back over in utter dismay, slapping one hand on the floor. The live audience went wild as Mr. Finch became the first person ever to posthumously win the Oscar for Best Actor. My father thought my reaction was hilarious; I was rooting pretty hard for Stallone, and Dad got a good, hearty laugh over my disappointment. It was a setback for my new favorite actor, but as a first-time nominee, he was up against some tough, sentimental competition.

Now the movie *Network* made me more anxious than ever. I really wanted *Rocky* to win that Best Picture award. Everyone was saying that *Network* was the hands-down favorite and *Rocky* was, of course, the underdog. I quietly watched the clips and waited for the next big announcement. Jack Nicholson took his place behind the podium and read the list of nominated movies. When he announced *Rocky* and they showed the clips, the camera went right to Stallone sitting in the audience. You could see him becoming very nervous. He looked like he was sweating it out, especially since he didn't win the Best Actor award. I wondered what he was thinking at that moment. To me he was Rocky sitting in that audience and I still thought of him as the underdog. *Network*, darn *Network*, that stupid movie is going to win.

I wasn't even considering such films as *All the President's Men, Taxi Driver* with some guy named DeNiro, plus *Bound for Glory*. I was only worried about *Network*. That was the one thing on my mind. Then that scary man named Nicholson with a voice that frightened me half to death finally said, "And the winner is *Rocky*, Irwin Winkler and Robert Chartoff producers."

The *Rocky* theme music kicked in, and it became another moment I'll never forget. I jumped up from the floor and nearly bounced off the low-tiled ceiling in our basement. As an Italian family of eight, we spent a lot of time living in our wood-paneled lower level.

"We did it!" I shouted.

Rocky had just won the Academy Award for Best Picture, and I felt like I was a part of it.

As the film's producers headed to the stage to receive their Oscars, they were first congratulated by Talia Shire, and then they grabbed Stallone and dragged him up with them. Like Rocky himself, the movie was a million-to-one shot to win—and it won! I couldn't wait to hear what Stallone, the actor with his growing fame minus his bow tie, would say to me and the American audience. I didn't remember his actual words, but through the magic of the 21st century, I found a recap on YouTube.com. Producer Robert Chartoff went first, and he said, "Sylvester Stallone, I would like to thank you for sharing your dream of *Rocky* with us and for giving us a performance that has enriched all our lives." That sentiment showed how one man's vision positively influenced many people around the world; Stallone's dream was his earthly mission.

Chartoff continued to thank the Academy for permitting *Rocky*, a long-shot underdog, to go the distance and win the Best Picture award. After Irwin Winkler spoke a few words of thanks, he turned it over to Stallone. I was listening intently as he bent toward the microphone and said, "And to all the Rockys in the world, I love you."

Stallone had figured it out again. There is a little Rocky in everyone, and love powers your heart and soul. I wonder if he could have ever imagined just how the movie would continue to influence my generation. The film was made out of love by the many people involved in the production. It was done with heart, as dollars didn't play much of a role in its success. That's why the original *Rocky* was so special and will forever stand out as the best film of the franchise.

As the three men walked off stage with their statuettes in hand, the *Rocky* theme song soared, and I was elated. Even my Dad was smiling. The night was complete. Rocky did it again, and I couldn't wait to call my friend Pete to share the victory with him. I knew that *Rocky* enthusiasts around the world were celebrating with us. That night solidified me as a fan forever. I've never rooted so hard, before or since, for a movie to win as I did for *Rocky*. It was the perfect Hollywood ending for a real-life situation.

The original film and the awards celebration became building blocks for my thought process and spirit at a perfect age. The experience laid the groundwork for my makeup and brought all of the motivating elements together, from spiritual energy to perseverance, desire and love. The sequels that followed continued to teach me life lessons that would later allow me to pursue my goals and someday help others do the same. This round, like in the early rounds of any fight, prepared me for what was needed as the inspiration to go the distance.

ROUND FOUR

Attracting a Goal

After *Rocky* won the Academy Award for Best Picture, all the kids in my neighborhood wanted to be a boxer or to train like one. We all had the soundtrack, either on vinyl LP records or 8-track and cassette tapes. My brother Sal would play the album, especially the theme song, "Gonna Fly Now," over and over again at the highest volume. Every last one of us in the neighborhood started some sort of workout routine, thanks to this movie. *Rocky* mania had definitely affected us in an extreme, high-energy way.

I can recall even the smallest detail of how this film became connected to my life and shaped my future journey. As an adult, I can see how all of the interesting tie-ins with family, friends, and experiences relate to my passion for it.

There were simple coincidences such as Talia Shire and I sharing the same birth date or that I had a childhood friend we called Spider, and Rocky's first opponent was named Spider Rico. Larger connections were present like the one between my godfather and Burt Young. They had been friends back in their younger days in their hometown. Burt actually installed a carpet in the upstairs apartment of my childhood house where my godfather lived.

I also learned that both of my parents knew Burt from the old neighborhood in Corona, Queens. My mother's grandparents competed with his family for the local bread business. The two families owned bakeries just blocks away from each other. Their hometown was a place where business was done locally, and everybody knew each other. Some of Burt's relatives actually became customers of my parent's home heating oil business. The connections continued to add up as they were pointed out to me.

I remember the first Rocky T-shirt I ever owned. I wore it for years until it finally fell apart. I think my mom might have been a bit smitten by Stallone and the movie because she bought me the shirt without me even asking for it. We purchased it on a weekend trip to visit family in, of all places, Rocky Point, Long Island. The light blue T-shirt had an iron-on picture of Rocky's face with a bruised eye.

I watched every second of the process of creating that shirt, as steam emanated from all sides of the machine. The unmistakable and distinct smell of an iron-on transfer being applied filled the air and I still remember it. I wore that T-shirt hundreds of times during my junior high school years until, eventually, it was shot full of holes. My friend Pete still reminds me about that T-shirt sometimes when we talk about *Rocky*. It's curious that I recall every detail about buying that shirt, but have no recollection of when I finally gave up on it; maybe that memory was blocked out on purpose.

Purchasing that T-shirt in Rocky Point along with some of the other tie-ins is an example of when the Law of Attraction started to manifest in my life. All things *Rocky* began to attract themselves to me, including a chance meeting with two of the main characters from the movie.

In 1978, with talk of *Rocky II* coming, another rumor hit our neighborhood. Burt Young and Talia Shire were scheduled to shoot a made-for-television movie for CBS titled *Daddy, I Don't Like It Like This* at a local corner eatery, the Lighthouse Diner which was directly around the block from my home.

One day a crowd of people gathered outside the diner with movie trucks and equipment in the background, confirming that two elements of *Rocky* would be live before my very eyes. I raced over with some friends and there I met Burt Young. It was after the first movie that I learned from my oldest brother Nick that Burt was a friend of my godfather, Norman. As I mentioned, they knew each other from the old neighborhood where Burt owned the ABC Carpet store across from Spaghetti Park, a local iconic destination. This was an incredible personal connection to one of my new favorite stars. Burt was the first actor I ever met in person; the second was the actress who played Rocky's girlfriend, Talia Shire.

I couldn't believe that I got close enough to speak to Mr. Young. I proudly shared my godfather and carpet story with him the minute I walked up to him. When he confirmed the stories were true, my friends were amazed and finally believed me about the connection. Suddenly the front doors of the diner opened and Talia Shire appeared.

I was astonished to see Adrian walking down the stairs. I couldn't believe it when Burt called her over and shared my carpet story with her. I was dumbfounded—Adrian was standing right there in front of me. She was gorgeous, and I was smiling from ear to ear. I nervously asked her for an autograph and she obliged. And then, to my total surprise, she kissed me on the cheek. It was a defining moment that I will never forget. I received a kiss from Adrian!

Later that year, *Rocky II* would be coming to the theaters, and I had just met two of the stars in person, right around the corner from my home. I couldn't believe my luck. I'm certain that Mr. Young had no idea of the major impression he made on me that day. His simple act of kindness solidified my good opinion of him and was probably one of the biggest factors, along with that peck on the cheek, of my growing fondness for the movie *Rocky*.

Ever since that day, I have also felt a unique affinity with Burt Young, and I hope he knows how his kindness affected the life of twelve-year-old boy through all these years. I still enjoy telling the story of our chance meeting.

The premiere of *Rocky II* was scheduled for June 1979. It would feature the big rematch between the Champion Apollo Creed and our favorite son, Rocky Balboa. I was delirious with excitement while watching the movie trailer in the theaters and commercials on television. I could hardly wait to see *Rocky II* and was counting the days till its release.

When opening day finally arrived, I made immediate plans to see it that night. I was standing in line with Sal and his girlfriend again; this time at the Main Street Theater, and we were pumped to see this sequel. The line on this opening night was longer than usual and a certain buzz was building up. The anticipation grew as we waited and strategized a plan for securing good seats. At one point, a car drove by the theater and someone yelled what turned out to be a false ending of the movie. Some people got upset and furious. I didn't appreciate the joke at first, but after seeing the movie, I thought the attempt at humor was pretty funny.

When the doors opened, we didn't even stop for popcorn because we had to rush in get our seats. It wouldn't have mattered anyway because while watching the original, most of the popcorn ended up on the floor during all of the action. Once seated, I was back in my comfort zone, in a giant-screen theater, just moments away from another round of *Rocky*. The house lights lowered, and we watched a series of previews, becoming more annoyed and impatient with each one. The anticipation and noise level were rising from the restless theater audience. When the trademark MGM Lion finally roared, the *Rocky* theme song started to blare, we knew the sequel of the century was on at last.

The relentless buildup of *Rocky II* was worth every second. The energy level escalated throughout the movie, as it featured one of the greatest endings of the entire series. The story began with the fight scene from the original and had everything you wanted and expected from a *Rocky* film. It included the always-exciting music, motivating training sequences, suspense, and the final, exhilarating fight scene. Most of our favorite characters returned to the big screen, including Rocky, Adrian, Apollo, Mick, and Paulie. The sequel also introduced Rocky Jr., a different cornerman (for some untold reason), plus a black satin tiger jacket, and a black and gold 1979 Trans Am (even though it was set in 1977).

Seeing this movie in the theater for the first time was another fantastic ride. My emotions raced from high, to low, and high again as I devoured every second of the film. There was a memorable proposal at the Philadelphia Zoo, their wedding, a failed attempt as a pitchman for a cologne company, the birth of their first child, and Adrian's unexpected coma. The hospital scene with Adrian was a little drawn out, but it was worth it when she woke up and asked Rocky to do one thing for her. She motioned for him to move closer and whispered, "Win." That simple word inspires me to this day.

During the big fight at the end of *Rocky II*, the audience reacted exactly as it had during the original. They leapt to their feet and cheered throughout the entire scene. I scrutinized every punch and was nervous about each knockdown. I lost myself in the drama and felt like I was in the movie, rather than just watching it. The whole time I wondered how it would end.

In anticipation of this film, I suspected that Rocky would win the rematch. But as I became engaged in the fight scene, I wasn't so sure. When this second fight also went to the fifteenth round, I figured it would end the same way as the original. The bell would ring, and Rocky would lose a decision once again. I prepared myself for the outcome, but held out hope that he would do it. At that exact moment, the exhausted Southpaw from Philly, who was fighting right-handed up until then, switched back to lefty at the urging of Mick, his manager. Rocky connected with a thunderous left to Apollo's chin, and I watched with eyes and mouth wide open as the champion fell to the canvas. But Rocky was falling even faster from the momentum of throwing the mighty blow. He had given it all he had. In slow motion, the challenger hit the canvas first, and the next thing I knew, both men were down.

The countdown started in slow motion with that famous echo: one ... two ... three ... three, three. This moment seemed to last a lifetime, and in retrospect, I guess maybe it did. The fighter who stands up before the count of ten is the champion. When referee Lou Filippo got to nine, a worn out Apollo Creed tried everything to get up, but he fell back down, sinking into the corner of the ring. What was going on? I was confused and about to crumble in exhaustion myself. Then I heard the referee continue, "Ten ... ten ... ten, you're out."

He waved his arms, and Rocky was the only one standing. The music started and so did the crowd frenzy—Rocky Balboa was the new Heavyweight Champion of the World!

It was like everyone in the theater had just won the big fight and pandemonium broke out once again. Strangers were hugging each other; some had tears rolling down their cheeks. This was the most powerful cinematic experience of my young life. The part that touched me most was when Rocky raised the championship belt in victory.

Once again, like in the original movie, the audience stood by their seats and read every credit. As we filed outside to the sidewalk afterward, everyone was shadow boxing again, and dancing in the street to the *Rocky* theme music they were singing. The atmosphere was electrifying, and there was a giant buzz. We all had a good laugh when some guy in a black and gold Pontiac Trans Am drove by screaming out his window and pumping his fist, "Rocky! Rocky! Rocky!" I vividly remember that moment, and I've always liked that car and thought, maybe someday I'll own one.

In the days after the opening of *Rocky II*, it seems most everyone in our town was obsessed with the new champion. My brother purchased some professional boxing gloves, and we had matches with kids from all over the neighborhood in our backyard. *Rocky* mania was running wild again, and we couldn't get enough of it. Most of us saw the movie numerous times in the theater, just like when the original came out. We all wanted to be just like Rocky. We wanted to follow his workout routine and be in shape like him. Most of us bought the soundtracks of both movies and played them over and over again. Rocky Balboa was the heavyweight champion, and all was right with the world. We were motivated by his success and believed that we could accomplish anything. *Rocky* truly was a part of the American culture, and for some of us, our makeup. If you lived through that time in the Seventies, this film probably impacted you in some way.

Most of us never noticed how dollars and cents took on more of a role in this production compared to the original. Stallone was a frequent guest on television shows and featured on magazine covers. Marketing of the film was ubiquitous. Gardner's Luncheonette sold the *Rocky II* bubblegum card series, and I collected every single one many times over. The card packs came with photo stickers, which I plastered on my bedroom walls and all over my school books. I discovered from one of those cards that Rocky's first name was actually Robert. The name was never said in any of the movies except when referring to his son and that became one of my favorite trivia questions.

After the phenomenal success of *Rocky II,* the character and the actor rode an even greater wave of popularity into the big-hair Eighties. The decade had a reputation of being excessive, and the *Rocky* franchise seemed headed in that direction. It strongly influenced me and introduced many new experiences into my teenage life. This exciting time also delivered a third round of *Rocky*.

In May 1982, *Rocky III* made its screen debut, and I was back in line at the UA Quartet for another exciting opening night. *Rocky* was bigger than ever and this new sequel promised to deliver an even larger punch. The stakes were raised, and a lot more money was invested in this film.

By then, I was on the road driving my own car, an old, red 1968 Mercury Montego MX that I purchased for five hundred dollars from the guy at our local gas station. It was a great car for a new driver and a kid my age. Although it wasn't in mint condition, I was grateful to have it.

So on opening night, I picked up Pete, and we drove over to the theater to see the new release. Watching a sequel on the first night was just the thing to do. The energy was always at its peak. Plus, I didn't want to give anyone a chance to talk about the movie in front of me and potentially ruin any part of it before having a chance to see it. That afternoon, I pre-purchased our tickets for the evening show in order to guarantee admission at night. It was another first, I never had to do this before.

Rocky III featured a lot of action, including plenty of fight and training scenes. It introduced new characters and unfortunately, an untimely death that really surprised me. I took it pretty hard when Mick died of a heart attack in this sequel. The loss of Rocky's loveable manager was a low point in the series, but on the other hand, seeing the champ team up with Apollo after losing the title to Clubber Lang was a good twist.

As the movie progressed, I was surprised to see Rocky given an opportunity to start all over again with his earlier opponent by his side. The old former champ took the new former champ back to his beginnings in Los Angeles to regain his motivation. Rocky had to overcome his inner demons of self-doubt. He became inspired to reclaim his championship desire and spirit. It got me thinking about what was important in life and taught me how to deal with loss and overcome it.

In the first two fights, Apollo Creed was respected as the charismatic champ and a popular character. When Rocky teamed up with him, their new goal was to both overcome losses in their lives. The passing of Mick seemed to take away Rocky's energy. His heart was being gut-checked and tested both in and out of the ring. Apollo tried to help Rocky regain his "Eye of the Tiger" while trying to overcome his own inner conflict regarding his lost title and the direction of his future.

As Rocky overcame his challenges in this film, he once again taught me another life lesson about the importance of rebuilding the heart of a champion. The Rocky Spirit continued to influence me on a whole new level as I was becoming a young adult. Through this film, I began to understand that when life takes you down and you experience loss, you are given two choices. You can either stay down, or you can pick yourself up and find a way back to the top. I relate this to God giving us the opportunity to seek the help we need to make the right decisions that determine our future. The film was molding me to become a disciple of the character Rocky.

Rocky III also introduced new characters like Hulk Hogan as ThunderLips and Mr. T as Clubber Lang. Hogan, whose real name is Terrance Bollea, was already known from his appearances in the World Wrestling Federation. There was no doubt that his career and Hulk-a-Mania skyrocketed into a new stratosphere after *Rocky III*. Sylvester Stallone and his team had a knack for choosing the right person for each role, which helped actors launch their careers and build their lives.

Mr. T (born Laurence Tureaud) was another fortunate person whose path crossed with Stallone. Cast as Clubber Lang, this strongman, former football player and bodyguard, scared the "you-know-what" out of me in *Rocky III*. At first glance, I knew Rocky would be in trouble. He played a great villain, and his character even shared some similarities with the original *Rocky* character when it came to determination. Stallone cast Mr. T after seeing him on a television program called *Games People Play*. He rode that same energy wave of *Rocky III* into a successful and long-running gig on *The A-Team* as B. A. Baracus. Now the *Rocky* movies were influencing the entertainment industry and the sport of boxing.

Stallone and the people behind him were building marketing machines with the sequels. The boxing and love story recipe was now taking a backseat to marketing and dollar signs. It didn't matter to me at the time because I just wanted to see more *Rocky*, along with anything else having to do with the franchise.

Rocky III delivered a musical hit with "Eye of the Tiger," which was highlighted on the soundtrack and performed by Survivor. The song was the band's most popular single and became an influential part of the Eighties decade. This sequel featured the most action and had me on the edge of my seat throughout.

Pete and I were already eager to see *Rocky IV*, which we knew would be coming out soon, especially considering how the third film had ended. After Rocky regained his title, with help from the former champ turned manager, Creed said that he owed him one in return for training him. That favor was to settle the previous fight that Rocky had won by just one second. The movie ended with the two great champions alone in a ring, throwing a simultaneous punch exchange that froze on the screen. I said to myself, *"Yes, another round of Rocky is coming. Bring it on!"*

As we waited for the next chapter of the series to come out, we were now able to watch the first three movies either on television or at home on a rented VHS tape in our new VCR. It was a whole new way to stay in touch with our favorite character and to see the films over and over again.

We continued to thrive on this movie franchise. In November 1985, I was now twenty-years old when *Rocky IV* was released. Once again, Pete and

I were in line for opening night along with another friend. As always, we were among the first to see it, and this one didn't let us down either. This sequel was known for several things, but it was the soundtrack that stole the show.

In *Rocky IV,* the champ tackled the story line of the Cold War between the United States of America and Russia. Rocky Balboa had always been an American hero, but this film made the character a bona fide icon.

Once again, Stallone made stars out of relative unknowns such as Dolph Lundgren, who portrayed the opponent Ivan Drago, and Bridgette Nielsen, who played his wife Ludmilla. Drago looked so massive and menacing that he came across as an unstoppable force. Nielsen was Stallone's current, off-screen girlfriend and would become his second wife. His personal life had gone in a new direction as his popularity skyrocketed, and he associated with some of the people who had attached themselves to him.

Rocky IV was one of the first films to insinuate the use of steroids in sports as Stallone continued to stay ahead of the curve. The unfamiliar use of drugs by athletes went over our heads back in the Eighties, and it was blunted by the excitement of another sequel. We didn't know it back then, but steroids played a parallel role in this film and in real life. Everything seemed bigger this time around, especially the dollars involved.

As a viewer, I was drained by all the high-powered action. This movie also brought the loss of another popular character when Apollo was killed in the ring by the oversized, chemically-enhanced, Russian fighting machine. We sat in total disbelief over this tragedy. The sequels were now building a tradition of personal loss for Rocky but they also showed how to overcome unbearable adversity.

One thing that remained true to form was the great music. Stallone and his team always managed to create the right music that would twist your emotions every which way. In the prior three films, Bill Conti gave us some legendary selections such as the inspiring theme song, "Gonna Fly Now." Frank Stallone delivered memorable versions of "Take You Back," and the band Survivor made history with "Eye of the Tiger." But the *Rocky IV* soundtrack took the franchise to a whole new level, leaving us pumped with unbounded energy.

We played that album over and over again back in the Eighties. Another close friend of mine, Joe, and I would blast it on our car radios at the highest possible decibel level. We used to cruise our identical red, 1971 Oldsmobile

Cutlass Supreme convertibles up and down the boulevard, and you could hear Vince DiCola's track, "War/Fanfare for Rocky," a mile away. People probably laughed at us, but we didn't care; we loved it and gloried in its pure, explosive energy.

We had great sound systems in those cars with high-powered speakers and power boosters that made the music so loud your ears would ring. One day I was parked in front of a store on the local main street with "War" blasting from the multiple speakers when someone knocked on my window. It was a store merchant complaining that my music was so loud she couldn't hear the customers inside her shop, and it was shaking her inventory off the shelves. She demanded that I move my car. I guess she was not a *Rocky* fan; she might have been the only one.

In my opinion, that is one of the best tracks of all time, and to this day, I still have to listen to it on the highest possible volume. Anytime I need an energy surge, I pop in the soundtrack, and I feel indestructible. *Rocky IV* was about the main character going global and solidifying his status as an American icon, but for me it was that soundtrack that stole the show.

Ironically, the film taught us we could do the impossible by staying clean and working hard. It reaffirmed the American spirit and gave us motivation and pride to carry on through the rest of the Eighties. Just like the other sequels, it continued to help me shape my own character. This movie was filled with energy, but it also gave us an opportunity to deal with the feeling of loss. Years later, in the next round of my life that lesson would be helpful to me.

ROUND FIVE

Measure of a Man

Toward the end of the decade, I graduated from college and started my career in the competitive business of radio advertising at a local station in the suburbs. I applied the same Rocky Spirit I had learned growing up to motivate myself to succeed in business; it was simply a part of my makeup.

The *Rocky* connections continued even as I started my first full-time job. I had a coworker with the last name of Stallone who became a good friend. She even sold me her white Pontiac Grand Prix when I needed a car. Stallone was her married name, and she was no relation to the actor, but these simple tie-ins kept following me around.

Being a kid from the big city, I felt lost on those first few days on the job in new surroundings. While driving around looking for a place to have lunch, I stumbled across Stallone's, an Italian fast-service restaurant. It was rumored that Sly, his mother Jacqueline and brother Frank, owned the franchise. Just the name alone made me feel at home, as I kicked off my adult life along with those additional *Rocky* connections.

Sequel after sequel, I became a bigger fan each time. In 1990, after most of us were convinced the series would end after the fourth film, we were treated to one more round, with *Rocky V*. This film never gets much respect from borderline fans because it strayed from the formula of the previous four. Some critics have questioned Stallone's reason for making *Rocky V*; was he just in it for another payday? Why didn't he direct it? What was the story behind getting his real-life son Sage involved? It was so different from the others that years later Stallone claimed he was not satisfied with *Rocky V* being the end of the saga. However, I think that true fans believe this film does find its place in *Rocky* history. Deep down I felt that it was a keeper because it contained familiar elements and saw the return of the character we first rooted for.

Even though *Rocky V* deviated from the original formula, it still had a lot to offer. Fourteen years later, this film took us back to South Philadelphia and taught me that it's all right to go home again, no matter what your status is in life. If they get knocked down, the great ones have the humble ability and heart to start over again to find their way back without ego.

After watching Rocky go over the top in the excessive Eighties, I liked seeing him get back to the old black hat, leather jacket and fingerless gloves in the Nineties. The film also introduced new talent, like Tommy Morrison as the young boxer Tommy Gunn and Richard Gant as George Washington Duke. Morrison was built for the part, being an up-and-coming heavyweight boxer in real life. Gant also did a great job portraying a fight promoter in the style of the flamboyant Don King. It also introduced a soundtrack featuring rap music, including artists MC Hammer, Rob Base, and Joey B. Ellis, to name a few. The *Rocky* franchise was again ahead of the times or at least right there with them.

The movies have always launched new ideas, careers, music, spiritual enlightenment and life lessons. One such lesson is epitomized in Elton John's "The Measure of a Man." That song lands solidly on my list of great *Rocky* tunes. It featured a strong message about rebounding from adversity. It is a measure of our spirit, explaining that the strong-minded will continue on. That selection has helped me through the low points of my career and life.

Rocky V was scheduled for release in November 1990, so Pete and I planned yet another opening night together, but this time we brought some tag-a-longs: his wife and an old girlfriend of mine.

After the four of us watched the movie that night, Pete and I came out of the theater pretty excited and pumped up. We had just learned another life lesson from our hero about staying true to our family and ourselves. We enjoyed it simply because it was Rocky back on the streets of Philadelphia where we first met him. The city takes you back to a familiar comfort zone. I'm not sure the girls were as thrilled as we were about the movie. A few days later, I saw it again with some friends from work because I knew I'd never get my girlfriend to sit through it twice.

At the conclusion of seeing it a second time, I realized how these movies continued to shape my outlook on life. I recall how the flashback of Mick telling Rocky "one more round" reverberated with me especially when I needed extra impetus to press on.

After *Rocky V*, I agreed with everyone that this was it; we had seen the last of the Italian Stallion. The saga had finally ended on the streets of Philadelphia as he walked away, not with the gold, but with his family, dignity and a blessing from Father Carmine. The following year, I often turned to nostalgia and the music to keep my Rocky Spirit alive. It would be used to motivate me through good times and in bad even as I was about to experience the toughest period of my young life.

In January 1992, I suffered the loss of my father after a four-month battle with lung cancer from cigarette smoking. My family and I watched him take his final breath and it was one of the most spiritual experiences ever. In a frozen moment, I reflected on the agonizing four-month battle that taught me about what is really important in life, but it was the hardest lesson that I had ever learned.

On a Sunday evening, in September 1991, my mother and father returned from a day-long visit to my sister's house. They came home in good spirits, but my mother began to discuss my father's erratic driving that evening. She mentioned that he was all over the road. I asked him if anything was wrong. He replied that he wasn't feeling right, was dizzy, and felt the pressure of an unusual headache. I will never forget offering him the simple advice of getting some sleep, saying that he would feel better in the morning. My mother suggested the same and said that if he did not, she would make an appointment with his doctor for a checkup. I didn't think anything of it. After all, we lived a life motto of "these things cannot happen to our family."

The next day at about 4 o'clock in the afternoon, our life would change forever. I received a telephone call at work from my sister Doreen telling me that the doctors found a tumor in my father's head. She said that they were putting him through additional tests and would call me later with more information. I tried going back to work but knew that I should be at the hospital to be with my father and family.

That night we spent many long hours waiting to hear an update. I remained positive, but around midnight the doctors informed us that my father had terminal lung cancer. We learned that tumors in his lungs were present and they had already spread to his brain and other parts of his body. The doctors said that we could see him but that we were not to mention the diagnosis. The experience of not saying anything was excruciating for us.

The next morning, I headed to the hospital to bring him a breakfast that my mother prepared. He was surprisingly talkative as I sat by his side. He began to discuss the diagnosis with me and asked if it was cancer. At that moment, I didn't say anything, as instructed, but knew that he got his answer from my eyes and body language. That afternoon, the doctors and my mother explained the diagnosis to him. Over the next four months we would watch my dad battle this incurable disease that would eventually take his life and our family's spirit.

Every week during his treatments we experienced various levels of emotions and always hoped for the best. Our family did whatever we could to support him while trying to continue our daily routines. On the days that he was admitted to the hospital, I would visit him in the mornings to bring him breakfast, whether he was able to eat it or not. While I sat with him, I got to learn about him in a way that he never shared before. I was extremely grateful to have those visits during his hospital stays.

When he was home during that time it was obvious how the treatments took their toll on him. Even though the diagnosis was not good, Dad decided that he would fight this illness hard and I believed that somehow he would win. We even saw some encouraging moments during the long battle.

Around Christmas time that year, he was holding steady as we were again grateful to share this holiday with him. We took this time as a family to reflect on how special these days really were. Shortly after the holiday while out for a walk with his brother, Dad suffered what appeared to be a seizure and collapsed. After a short hospital stay, he was sent home to share his final days with us. Over the next three weeks, we all got to see what this terrible disease could do as it whittled away at this once strong man. My sisters cared for him every last second as my mother prepared for the inevitable. My brothers manned the family business with great dignity and I did whatever was possible to lend support while trying to cope with this devastating and life-changing time for all of us.

During the very last days of his four-month battle, my sister Doreen, with gracious help from hospice, made his final time comfortable and calm in a makeshift hospital in the middle of our living room. My sister always had a special connection to him and communicated with him throughout, even though he was in and out of consciousness. She knew what was coming and tried her best to also keep everyone else calm.

On a Tuesday morning in late January the time had arrived. The weather was cloudy that day as I prepared to head out for work. I began to hear nervous activity with the door bell constantly ringing and people entering the house. My sister had called our local parish for a priest. When he arrived, we were all called up to Dad's bedside to spend the last few precious moments of his life with him. We were about to become introduced first-hand to the meaning of death.

Someone's passing can rarely be described as spectacular, but what we witnessed that morning was one of the most spectacular images that I have ever seen even through the sorrow of losing our father. As the room darkened from the cloudy morning, the priest gave us all a moment to hold Dad's hand and share an everlasting touch as he fought through grim, shallow breathing with his eyes closed. After that brief interaction, the priest then stepped over to Dad's bed and administered last rites as we kneeled by his side.

As the very last word was spoken and the Sign of the Cross was presented over him, our father, with every last bit of strength and will, opened his eyes wider than I had ever seen them before. They looked like giant white globes of glistening light as he looked at all of us one by one to say goodbye, telling us that he loved us and it was all right for us to press on. His last vision of his life was a message of love.

One small tear of strength rolled down his face from his right eye as he breathed in and exhaled for the very last time. Our father had passed on before our very eyes. At the exact moment of his final breath, the once dreary morning sky broke open and brilliant beams of sunlight began to shine directly on him through the front bow window of our home. It lit up the room in a warm and spectacular way that left us all aghast. I recall looking up at the rays of sun as a stairway to the heavens.

Spectacular, yes it was. It is truly the only respectful word to describe this extremely spiritual moment. Through his passing and lengthy battle with the illness, he taught us a final lesson about strength, dignity and the importance of family. It also made me understand the powers from above, as the experience opened my awareness to spirituality. Our father wanted to live and he fought valiantly, but his illness was advanced. It took his life, but not his everlasting spirit that was gracefully shared with all of us that morning.

In spite of the lessons my father's passing taught me, it was a confusing time. I put my personal life on hold, and my career suffered as I struggled to find my way. I found myself knocked down on the canvas during this round with no drive to get up and move on. My concentration level slumped and I felt distracted. I even had a few car accidents that year, which continued to set me back. It was a low-energy time of my life.

Late one night after dropping off a friend out east, I was heading back home driving westbound on the parkway around 2 a.m. Apparently I nodded off briefly, just minutes from my destination. When I opened my eyes, my vehicle was swerving toward the center guard rail. Startled awake, I applied fast, strong pressure on the brake pedal, steering hard in the opposite direction. My car at the time, a mint-condition 1988 Pontiac Bonneville SSE, slid sideways across three lanes of highway. The front end struck a tree on the passenger side and then slammed into another guard rail. In what felt like slow motion, my car rolled over the rail and I was thrown out of my seat, landing upside down, eventually sitting inside of the car on the sunroof. I was dazed and confused, but surprisingly unharmed. A rear wheel was still spinning, making a loud hissing noise. I thought my car was going to explode. I was scared, but got my bearings and acted quickly while figuring out an escape route. I crawled out of the broken driver's side window and got out of danger without a scratch.

I have always wondered what protected me that night. There I was, upside-down in a ditch with extensive damage to my car; but I felt a presence watching over me, even sitting next to me. I sensed a strong force in the passenger seat with a hand on my shoulder throughout the terrifying incident. Was I just lucky or did something else shield me that strange morning on the road?

In the fall of that same year, I experienced another freak accident when a woman's car spun out of control across a major roadway, causing a head-on collision with mine. This time I was not so lucky. Serious neck and back injuries disabled me and kept me out of work for the next four months. Life was certainly taking me down a difficult path, and I faced some real adversity. I was at a crossroads and had to make a choice. I could have given up, stayed down for the count, and accepted defeat. Instead, I chose to find my inner Rocky Spirit. I decided to press on as my father willed, work hard to rebuild myself and set goals to achieve at the highest level.

A turning point came when I managed to attend our company holiday celebration later that year, even though I was still out on sick leave. Our company sales manager, a gentleman named Charlie, was a legendary media salesperson with great street instincts and a sense of humor. I looked up to him and respected his advice. He was the only person at work that I confided in during the months of my father's illness and one of the first people I called after Dad passed away.

Charlie took me aside at the event and gut-checked me. He knew that certain issues were bothering me, especially with the loss of my father still fresh in my mind. He didn't show pity, but offered some quality advice that shook me up. He said I had too much potential and implored me to get my act together, to work hard, and get back into shape. He even told me to get a haircut. He said I should go back to just being myself, to become the man I was meant to be. That's when I began to rebuild my body, mind and soul. Charlie's words and the Rocky Spirit once again motivated me to fight hard and take on life again. I chose to use my setbacks as inspiration. It was that inner strength to never to give up, a quality I had always associated myself with, just like a favorite movie character of mine. I used Charlie's wakeup call to get myself back on track in all facets of my life.

Experiencing personal loss and a lack of wholeness becomes a defining time in your existence. It alters your thought process and could potentially keep you down if you let it beat you. Personal loss does take time to figure out in order to re-awaken positive energy to get back on your feet. I chose to get stronger both physically and emotionally. I managed to get back up on the canvas before the ten count to recapture solid footing. I refused to be defeated and kept hearing Mick say, "One more round. I didn't hear no bell."

ROUND SIX

Is it the Law of Attraction?

The new year held great promise. By 1993 I had rebounded and was once again myself. I began rebuilding my sales career, hitting the pavement hard with revitalized energy and spirit. New opportunities came at me from every direction, including a business deal with a local nightclub called The Dublin Pub.

They hired me to do a four-week promotion as the host of their famous Ladies Night on Thursdays. I also handled the prize giveaways to the bar patrons. My second week there, I met a girl named Chrissy while handing out roses as part of that night's giveaways.

When she turned to look at me, I was dazzled by her mass of curly blond hair, blue eyes, and terrific smile—she had it all. I gave her every last one of my giveaways that night. Several years later, this beautiful girl became my wife, and I'm still giving her everything.

Within a few weeks of meeting her, we were dating regularly, and my future began to manifest and take on a new direction. Through a connection with her energy and motivated by her love, positive experiences began to happen for me. It also felt like Chrissy had always been part of my *Rocky* experiences. To this day, I'm not exactly sure if she's a bona fide fan of the films, but she knows what they mean to me. She supports me through the ups and downs of all of my adventures.

One time we took a trip to an outlet mall in Reading, Pennsylvania. After our shopping excursion, I talked her into helping me find the Rocky Steps in Philadelphia. That was one place I had always wanted to visit. Apparently I never had the right map reader in the passenger seat until I met her. The spontaneity of this unplanned trip made the anticipation of finally arriving there so much more exciting. Somehow we located the cathedral-like steps without the benefit of a cell phone, the Internet, or a GPS, since those gadgets were not yet common or available. I just needed Chrissy by my side to navigate.

We parked the car in a big lot across the street from the Philadelphia Museum of Art and the steps just beyond. I was speechless as we approached the equestrian monument of George Washington. Yes, I was a kid in the candy store once again as I readied myself for this first memorable run up those steps. I wondered what Chrissy was thinking. She seemed excited, but I bet she was hoping I wouldn't embarrass her. We snapped a lot of pictures until we were finally ready for our run.

Of course, the *Rocky* theme song was going through my mind as I charged up the magnificent flight of sacred stone. I also wondered if people at the top would make fun of me when I jumped around pumping my fists high in the air. But that didn't stop me. Reaching the top of those steps with this girl was a symbol that I was all the way back. A mysterious energy ensued as I thrust my arms skyward. It was my first visit to this iconic location and Chrissy shared in the positive energy that surrounded us.

Afterward, we took a moment to sit there and watch a lot of other people do the very same thing, jumping up and down with raised fists. This confirmed that the steps are truly a special place. There's a reason why millions of people from all over the world are drawn to them. By running those steps, I accomplished something I had always wanted to do; it was truly energizing.

Chrissy and I had many memorable experiences in the mid-Nineties. We lived a busy and fun-filled dating life. I still managed to keep up on any *Rocky* news that came my way. In 1996, I read that some of the original cast of the film would be making a 20th anniversary appearance at a special party in Manhattan. It would take place at the Official All-Star Café in Times Square. The sports-themed restaurant was an offspring of Planet Hollywood, which was founded by Robert Earl, former president of the Hard Rock Café. It was endorsed and backed by Sylvester Stallone, Bruce Willis, Demi Moore and Arnold Schwarzenegger.

I really wanted to attend this event. Since I was working in the radio business at the time, I could have used my media connections to get me there, but for some reason I never pursued it. It may have had something to do with an incident that was experienced earlier that year.

Chrissy and I were out enjoying a fun night in Manhattan with friends. As we walked past the Official All-Star Café, we overheard people saying that Heavyweight Champion Evander Holyfield was about to exit the restaurant. We stopped to see what was going on and maybe catch a glimpse of the celebrity, but we were forced back by security goons. They kept pushing everyone behind the ropes that were not close to the action. Sometimes bodyguards take themselves too seriously and forget it's the fans that make these people famous. No one else was pushing or shoving except for them. Their hostile attitude was uncalled for. It left a negative impression on me that carried over into my *future* decision not to participate in the *Rocky* anniversary event. The negative thought process in this Law of Attraction example would trigger a negative result but, like they say, things happen for a reason.

My unpleasant experience that night led me to imagine what it might be like to attend the *Rocky* promotion. Would I once again be pushed behind some ropes and stuck nowhere near the action? I'm a guy who needs to be right in the middle of it, such as in the front row at a big fight. So I chose not to attend the 20th anniversary reunion at the Official All-Star Café—a decision I would later regret.

Afterward, I saw pictures and a recap of the party online. All of the celebrities were smiling and seemed to be having a wonderful time. That's when I realized I should have done whatever it took to attend, and it started to bother me. I mentioned to Chrissy that of all the *Rocky* fans in the world, I believed I was the one who really should have been there.

The smart marketing people took advantage of the occasion and released a special 20th anniversary VHS collection of the *Rocky* series. The boxed set, which I purchased from Costco that holiday season, came with a small souvenir booklet with photographs from the event that portrayed it as a glamorous affair. I began to brood over how I had missed my chance to participate. The disappointment stayed with me for a long time.

I mentioned to Chrissy that if they ever did another promotion like that again, there was no way I would miss it. I was determined to do whatever it took to be there. I don't think she was even listening to me when I made that vow, but she knew that missing that event bothered me.

It seems like when things don't go your way, it's because something better is waiting for you down the road—as long as your thoughts remain positive. I truly believe that I was meant to miss that event because it ignited my motivation and ultimate drive for future opportunities. I kept saying over and over again that I would be there for the next one; the only question was: Would there ever be another chance? I continued though to keep the Rocky Spirit in my life.

Chrissy and I were married in December 1997. The planning of our wedding was a lot of fun, but also stressful, as everyone had warned us it would be. Another *Rocky* tie-in occurred when we met the bandleader and DJ we hired to perform at our wedding. In selecting the music for our reception, I requested a special song for the entrance of the bride and groom. I wanted them to play the *Rocky* theme song "Gonna Fly Now." The bandleader refused because he had his own signature entrance song and he insisted that he had a much better selection for the occasion. I couldn't believe this guy. I was paying for his services and he was arguing with me? He looked over at Chrissy to plead his case, but she just chuckled and pointed a finger to the side of her head and moved it in a circular motion to indicate I was crazy. She gave my song choice her blessing, and he wrote "Rocky Theme Song" on the contract. The battle was won. However, the bandleader didn't go down easy. When he introduced us and the band started to play "Gonna Fly Now" he had to say "Entering to this song by request of the groom." I guess he was covering his back in case it didn't work, and then he could say it was my fault.

I can't speak for my wife, who sort of puts up with my idiosyncrasies, but entering that room to the *Rocky* theme song was exhilarating. It was a huge high for me, and everyone seemed to love it. When some of our guests echoed that sentiment, I knew that we had made an excellent choice.

Weeks later, when we picked up our wedding video, the videographer showed us some cool animations he had inserted to make it play like a motion picture. Seeing this instantly gave me an idea, and my wife braced herself because she knew exactly what I was going to say, even though we had never discussed it.

"Would it be possible to start the video like the movie *Rocky* with our names scrolling across the screen?"

He said he'd never done anything like that before, but he'd give it a try. When my wife agreed to the idea, I knew once again that I married the right girl. So with a few extra bucks, our wedding video now bursts into action to the tune of "Gonna Fly Now" with our names scrolling across the screen. Even people who don't get the whole *Rocky* thing enjoy the beginning of it. You don't have to be a fan to recognize that theme song and its powerful meaning; it has become a universal form of higher energy. Every step of my life held a little bit of the Rocky Spirit that continued to manifest in me.

After our wedding, my *Rocky* adventure of a lifetime began to take off. We moved into a two-bedroom apartment on the second floor of a private house. My wife gave me permission to set up my computer in one bedroom and use it as an office. To make it my own, I proudly placed my *Rocky* 20th anniversary VHS collection on the top shelf of a cabinet with glass doors as I began to build my environment. That VHS collection always reminded me of what I missed out on and fueled my desire for that next opportunity.

Above my computer was an empty space on the wall suitable for hanging a framed picture. I knew what I wanted to put there, but never found anything that would work. One day while walking through the mall, I stopped at one of those kiosk booths that sell memorabilia and movie posters. I was filing through a large batch of inventory when the clerk asked if he could help with something.

I said that I was looking for a photograph from the movie *Rocky*. The guy said he had only one, and it was from *Rocky II*. It featured the Italian Stallion in his black and yellow shorts and Apollo in red and white, taking a punch to the face. The Internet was only starting to get popular at that time, and you didn't see much *Rocky* memorabilia around. I quickly decided to purchase the photograph. The next day, I found the perfect black frame with a gold border and hung it above my computer facing the doorway, so I could see it whenever I passed by.

I didn't realize it at the time, but not only did I purchase one of the most significant pieces of my memorabilia collection, it turned out to be the exact item that would help me manifest the rest of my journey. Because of this photograph, I began to dream again about being in a *Rocky* movie. One day, I stopped to study it up close and noticed one particular gentleman sitting in the corner of the ring in the front row as a spectator. The movie extra looked like John Denver, the popular country music singer whose most famous hit single was ironically "Rocky Mountain High."

What is John Denver doing at the filming of *Rocky*, I wondered in jest?

How did this guy get a front row seat? Every time I looked at the photo, the John Denver look-alike would catch my eye, and I thought how cool it would be if I were that guy in the front row at the filming of a fight scene in a *Rocky* movie. I wanted to be that person. In my mind, I started to plant the seed of intention toward a future goal on my ladder of success. It became a daily mantra every time I looked at the picture: *"That should be me in the front row of a fight scene."*

I repeated that every day for two years before covering the picture with bubble wrap for the move to our new home, where it ended up in a bin in the attic as part of my memorabilia collection. But that image stuck in my head. I was determined to be the guy in the front row of a *Rocky* movie. When we moved into our house, Chrissy said no *Rocky* photos allowed, but I did manage to sneak in a poster that I hung up in the garage.

My obsession continued to grow after I purchased that photograph. One day I logged on to a new Web site that people were talking about called eBay. Naturally, the first thing I searched for on this buying and selling site was *Rocky* memorabilia. I typed "Rocky Stallone" into the search feature, and much to my delight, there was so much merchandise that I couldn't resist. I immediately signed up and created an account.

After seeing all the cool things to purchase, I just went for it. When I originally signed up for an America Online account in the mid-Nineties, I was lucky to get the e-mail address RockyBalboa1@aol.com, but when I tried for "Rocky Balboa" as my account name on eBay, it was already taken, so I settled on one that was very similar.

Signing on to eBay turned me into a fanatic *Rocky* collector. Over the years, I purchased just about everything that was for sale during the successful run of the franchise. There wasn't much available from the original movie. I read somewhere that Stallone regretted not taking full advantage of merchandising the film as much as he could have. He should have gone to the Disney school of promotions.

There are probably still some great old pieces of memorabilia out there, but either I haven't come across it yet, or it's something I refuse to overpay for. Part of the intrigue of collecting is acquiring that hard-to-find item at an incredible deal. One of my first eBay purchases was winning a Rocky pencil-top eraser. I never stopped shopping after making that purchase. Whenever a package arrived in the mail, my wife would say, "Not another stupid *Rocky* toy." Deep down, I know she really gets it, even though she enjoys harassing me.

With my new hobby of shopping on the Internet, I was now open to tons of *Rocky* information. I could buy books and check out Web sites to read about the actors and what it was like to be a part of the franchise. The Internet reinforced my fascination, and together with missing the anniversary event and concentrating on the photograph, the Law of Attraction continued to manifest future connections.

Life was moving fast as the decade and century came to an exciting close and a new millennium was filled with promise. The year 2000 was one of the best ever for me. We moved into a new home—which took forever, not only to find, but also to win in a bidding war—with the housing boom in full swing. The economy was strong, there was plenty of money to be made, and I took full advantage of it as things started to fall into place.

In late January, I received the greatest news ever: I was going to be a father for the first time. Chrissy wrote a note that began with "Dear Daddy" and she handed it to me one night after coming home from work. It puzzled me at first, but once I figured out what it meant, I could not believe it. For me to be given the privilege to be a dad was a blessing. I was extremely grateful to Chrissy and anticipated our future parenthood together. We looked forward to starting our family and wondered what the gender of our newborn baby would be. My life was energized by knowing that I was going to become a father.

Our daughter was born in September that year. When we were trying to come up with names prior to her birth, I threw Adriana into the mix, which was no surprise to Chrissy. That name had stuck in my head because of the wedding scene in *Rocky II*. The priest, Father Carmine, had called the bride by her full name Adriana Pennino in such a charming Italian accent that the first name stuck with me. We strongly considered it for our baby, but because of a situation with one of our friends we eventually decided on Gina Marie, a classic Italian name. I became a dad to our beautiful little girl: a gift from God. It was one of the most meaningful years of my now busy and responsible life. I wondered if Gina would be a future *Rocky* fan.

In the summer of 2002, we took a vacation to Hershey Park in Pennsylvania. My family was too excited to realize that I had a little scheme going on in the back of my mind. On the way home, I once again negotiated with Chrissy for another trip to the Rocky Steps. I admit to having a one-track mind, but this time I wanted to give my daughter a real-life *Rocky* experience. Even though she was young, she was of course familiar with the movies and was certainly familiar with the Rocky Steps.

My wife was then pregnant with our second child so she wasn't very enthusiastic about going, but I appreciated that she agreed. We will never forget the sight of our little girl chugging up those steps, holding her daddy's hand. When we got to the top, she knew exactly what to do. She stood next to me and raised her arms in the victory stance. I must say, it was one of the cutest scenes ever. Gina Marie stole the show, and every person there melted when they saw her do the Rocky pose. I took a photo of her alone on the top of the steps that I will cherish forever as one of those special moments frozen in time.

Our second daughter was born in December, and with Adriana still fresh in our minds, we agreed that this would be her name. However, when it came down to signing the birth certificate papers, we did have a slight moment of hesitation. We had selected two names for our new baby girl: Adriana and Christina. One would be the first name, and the other would be her middle name. We were about to make a lifetime decision, so we took a minute to think about it and began to second-guess ourselves as to which name would come first. Chrissy liked the name Adriana and she remained supportive of it. When it came down to making the final decision, we turned to Gina Marie, the new big sister.

"What is your little sister's name?" we asked. "Is it Adriana or Christina?"

Gina Marie was just two years old, and without hesitation, she smiled at us and said in her adorable voice, "Adriana, her name is Adriana," like it was meant to be.

So that was it, Gina Marie chose her name, and we had our precious baby Adriana. We even pronounced it with an Italian accent, just like good old Father Carmine. It was the perfect name for a perfect girl.

These special times, especially with the birth of our children, were all a part of life's journey. Each moment ignited energy vibrations that always would lead to a next step. Even though change was always present, the connections to a childhood memory remained with me through every round of my story.

ROUND SEVEN

Manifesting the Opportunity

As life got busier with two small children, I embarked on a new career when my current radio company started a weekly newspaper. We brought back the old *Long Island Press,* a throwback to the heritage name of the daily newspaper that I delivered for my brother as a kid. It was the publication that I used to look up show times for the original *Rocky* movie. I guess becoming a newspaper man may also have happened for a reason.

Even as I took on a new career challenge, I still managed to keep my *Rocky* collection growing. When buying toys for my daughters online, I usually found a collectible or two on eBay for myself. Somehow I found the time and money to purchase some cool new items.

Surfing the Internet, I stumbled on a rumor that Sylvester Stallone was interested in making *Rocky VI*. I checked on it, but it remained just that: an on-again, off-again rumor for the next year or two. Each time the issue came up in conversation with anyone, I would mention that if *Rocky VI* ever became a reality, I intended to find a way to be a part of it. In my mind, I was already there.

Many years after *Rocky V* hit the big screen, speculation continued to circulate that Stallone was working on another script. I read that he was not satisfied with how the last film had left the character, but he never confirmed anything about another sequel.

The rumors would come and they would go; one day it was true, and the next day it was not. For me at least, it offered a glimmer of hope that another *Rocky* experience could be just down the road. I reminded Chrissy that if *Rocky VI* became a reality, I would find a way to be an extra in that movie. I rambled on in affirmation, "I will be in that movie, no doubt about it; I will be in that movie when they do it."

She would laugh, or even ignore me, but I kept repeating the mantra in a purposeful way, as if it had already happened. Every time I brought up the possibility of being in a *Rocky* movie, I thought about that guy in the old picture who looked like John Denver. Could I really do it? First, I always confirmed it with a yes, but suspicion still lingered that Hollywood just might be out of reach, even for a great networker like me. However, that sentiment only fueled my motivation. Tell me I can't do something, and I will fire back with some quick action to prove that I can. I told myself, of course I would be in that movie, if they ever decide to make it.

For years, as the rumors continued, I truly believed that one day it would happen. I continued to visualize myself in the same seat as that guy. The rumor heated up in late 2004, and I continued to keep an eye on the situation. The next year, it got closer to being a reality as interviews with Stallone had him saying that an additional sequel needed to be made because he didn't like the way *Rocky V* ended.

Everyone who knew me mentioned the buzz they'd heard. I never realized how many people actually paid attention; I guess we all grew up with *Rocky*. You might be surprised at the number of people who, deep down, know and like the character and are fans of the movie in some way. They were all helping me affirm that something special was going to happen. Each time I heard the rumor from someone or somewhere, my wife would be reminded of my promise to be a part of the next movie.

MGM, Sony Pictures and Paramount finally struck a deal with Stallone to give him the funding and go-ahead to begin production in 2005. *Rocky VI* was officially on, even though Stallone was in his late fifties by then. When the announcement was made, I learned that it would not be a numbered sequel like the previous ones; the title would be *Rocky Balboa*.

Once again, everybody told me the movie was going to happen and joked about Stallone's advancing age. I was a *Rocky* magnet and felt great to be associated with it. As I mused about the reality of *Rocky Balboa*, I was convinced of my destiny to be a part of this movie adventure. I had been talking about it for years, and now it was finally official. It was "game on."

Every night I searched online for anything *Rocky*, looking for tidbits about the movie. I fantasized about participating in the fight scene, but having visited Philadelphia twice now, I believed I could fit in anywhere; I didn't care where. However, my Internet searches were coming up empty, and I began to fear that Hollywood was slipping from my grasp. With no real connections, how was I going to navigate this dream? But I never gave up. Like a fighter against a dangerous opponent, I kept on trying. I often repeated to myself that quote from Mick "I didn't hear no bell; one more round."

I continued to search for information, and told everyone about my quest and goal to be in *Rocky Balboa*. Many people listened and nodded politely. Feigning interest, they walked away, probably to smirk and mock me behind my back.

Every Wednesday night was the publication deadline for the *Long Island Press* and I always worked late. It gave me a chance to do my Internet searches and discuss them with my friend Danny, the general manager of the newspaper. Danny was a focused guy who kept a close eye on the progress of our new product. He would push me to work harder to succeed. Sometimes he would look at me with disdain when I talked about *Rocky*. He knew me well enough to be convinced that I was certifiably nuts.

"Please stop it with that *Rocky* stuff," he often said. "We have to concentrate on building a newspaper." I just nodded, smiled and quietly continued my research.

I would tell everyone about my goal, even though I suspected no one ever listened to me. One day, however, one of the all-around greatest guys in the world, another coworker and friend, Harlan, showed me that he was paying attention. We had worked together for many years. In 2005, he was in the radio division of our company as I was in the publishing division. Harlan often stopped by my desk to talk a little *Rocky* with me. He once took a trip to Philadelphia and brought me back a Rocky refrigerator magnet as a souvenir. Harlan is a thoughtful gift giver and a real good man. He appreciates the *Rocky* franchise and has been an avid fan his whole life. He was just as excited as I was that *Rocky Balboa* was going to be a reality.

Why do I bring up Harlan? His actions were pivotal in helping me turn my mission into a reality. It was a Wednesday afternoon in October when my computer went "ding," signaling an incoming e-mail from him. I was electrified when I saw the subject line: "Casting call for *Rocky* extras."

I scanned the information about the filming of a fight scene in Las Vegas. It explained that a company called BeInAMovie.com was looking for people to be unpaid extras for the new *Rocky* movie. Volunteers could sign up on their Web site.

My adrenaline surged as I clicked on the link; it was overwhelming. I was, of course, skeptical about it. I needed time to pore over the fine details, so I clicked off and forwarded the message to my home e-mail address. It was too intense for me to concentrate on at work. I would research the Web site thoroughly at home before registering and giving up any personal information. I do admit, I must have clicked on that link about a hundred times that afternoon to look at it.

I dashed up the stairs to Harlan's office at the radio station on the second floor. He had a huge grin on his face, and I could tell he was pretty excited about discovering this important piece of information for me. I asked if it was a legitimate Web site and how he found it. He explained that being the program director of a radio station, he often received press releases like that from people hoping he would talk about their cause on air. He told me not to worry, it was for real. "Go for it!" he said. That was all the encouragement I needed, and I couldn't thank him enough for the heads-up. Harlan called everyone "Buddy" and I can still hear him saying, "Good luck with it, Buddy."

When I got home that night, I couldn't wait to check out BeInAMovie.com and to reassure myself that it was the real deal. I also realized that this was my best, and probably only, shot. I didn't think twice about it. If you want to make something happen, you have to take action—so I did. I signed up to be an unpaid extra in the fight scene of *Rocky Balboa*. It would take place in two months at the Mandalay Bay Hotel and Casino in Las Vegas that December.

The Web site explained that I should not sign up for the opportunity unless I could guarantee to be there for one entire day. It stated that if I were selected, they would e-mail all the necessary details and information. It was getting more exciting every second. I signed myself up and even registered Chrissy without her knowledge or permission. I knew she wouldn't mind a trip to Las Vegas.

The site said that I'd be informed within three days if selected. The very moment I hit the send button, I began daydreaming about appearing in the film. That was the only thing on my mind as I drifted off to sleep that night. Could this be true? Would I really be flying off to Las Vegas to be part of the fight scene in the final *Rocky* movie?

The next day, Harlan buzzed in to ask if I had followed through with the sign-up process. "Absolutely," I said, explaining every detail to him.

"Good luck, Buddy," he replied again.

That boosted my confidence, and I believed my chances were good. I checked my e-mail every few minutes and went on BeInAMovie.com to read and research about a hundred more times that day. It was all I could think about. The anticipation was killing me. Danny admonished me to get my head out of the clouds and concentrate on my sales gig; we were trying to build a newspaper here. He kept prodding, and I kept nodding as I returned to my desk. I did, of course, continue to check my e-mail throughout the day.

That night, I filled Chrissy in on what was happening. She was also skeptical at first, as I figured she would be, but I could see she was a little excited about the opportunity. I could tell she was glad that I had signed her up. I'd been saying for years that I wanted to do this, so she knew there was no stopping me now. She knows how dangerous I can be when I put my mind and my full attention to something, especially if that something comes from my heart and soul. I have tremendous confidence that I can accomplish anything I set my mind to.

Sure enough, that night it came. The e-mail I was anticipating arrived from someone named Cash at BeInAMovie.com. The subject line announced I had been accepted, so that was excellent news. My heart started to race and I felt a tremendous energy rush.

When I opened the e-mail and learned that we both were accepted, I jumped out of my chair. The message contained all the important and necessary information about the filming of the fight scene. It would take place from Saturday December 3rd through Friday December 9th at the Mandalay Bay Hotel & Casino. It allowed us to select one day on-set, with Tuesday being the biggest day when they would need the most people. I was instructed to reply regarding my availability and which day I had chosen.

The e-mail employed a scare tactic, stating that once I committed to a date, I had to guarantee to show up. If I didn't, I would be banned from any future opportunities on their Web site. This all was so new to me and a bit overwhelming, but when I got over the initial excitement of being selected, it was once again "game on." I could step back and put it all together logically.

The Law of Attraction explains that everything you need to transform your thoughts into reality already surrounds you, and this opportunity was becoming a text-book example. The fight scene was to take place in Las Vegas, and it just so happened that a year earlier, my sister Angela, her family and my mother had moved, of all places, to Las Vegas. Everything was falling into place—it was too perfect. I called my sister to explain what was happening and asked if we could bring the kids out to stay with her family. Angela agreed to my plan and laughed because she also knows what I can accomplish when I put my mind to something. She fully understands my passion for these films.

The wheels were turning; I now had a purpose and a clear goal. December's calendar was jam-packed with special events: the trip to Las Vegas, Adriana's birthday, our wedding anniversary, and, of course, Christmas. Money was definitely a consideration in making these plans.

This is how the Law of Attraction continued to manifest as my family members came through for me again. My brother-in-law Joe, who is married to my middle sister Doreen, had recently taken a job at JetBlue Airways. I remembered hearing him talk about free airplane tickets called buddy passes once and had stored that information for a potential future request. After taking care of the lodging arrangements with Angela, I immediately called Doreen and explained my *Rocky* opportunity. I wondered if her husband could possibly provide eight buddy passes for my family to fly roundtrip to Las Vegas. I knew that was a lot to ask, but I had a game plan and was determined to work it out. Without hesitation she said yes, and everything continued to flow smoothly. I could feel her excitement right from the start. Doreen was thoroughly aware of my *Rocky* passion, and she understands drive, determination and goal-setting better than anybody I know. She's been through a lot in her life, and I know she has that Rocky Spirit in her, too. In fact, I probably acquired some of those traits from her as a kid. I always paid attention and learned from my brothers and sisters, which for me was one of the benefits of being the youngest of six children.

Once my travel arrangements were completed, I turned my attention to explaining every exciting detail to Chrissy. The e-mail said I could select only one day for both of us to be on set at the Mandalay Bay. When it was over, we could sign up for one additional day if they needed more extras, so I began to formulate a strategy. I selected Monday because I figured we stood a better chance of landing the additional day on Tuesday, when they needed the most people. It was the perfect plan. I sent back the request and spent the rest of the night trying to convince myself I'd made the right choice.

The next day, Cash at BeInAMovie.com confirmed by e-mail that we had been approved for Monday. My mind continued to work overtime as I put together the rest of my plan. Since I could use this trip as a family getaway, I wanted to extend my time in Las Vegas as much as possible. We would leave Friday afternoon, December 2nd, so we could spend all of Saturday with my sister to celebrate her birthday. We would remain in Las Vegas until the following Wednesday. Taking a deadline day off from work was most unusual for me, but this was about Rocky, so I took my chances. It was the opportunity of a lifetime and I had to believe that my company would understand. I definitely wanted to return by Thursday so my fantasy trip wouldn't interfere with my real-life responsibilities.

I still had to pick up the buddy passes from my brother-in-law, make the airline reservations and officially inform my job about my schedule, which I did the next day. Most of the final details were now in place. I knew what time we were leaving, who was babysitting for my daughters, ground transportation, and most of the instructions for being on the set of *Rocky Balboa*. The only thing left was to discuss with my wife whether to reserve an overnight stay at the Mandalay Bay so I could be close to the action and not miss anything. We decided yes, even though we didn't want to spend the extra money. In hindsight, it turned out to be a smart move due to the long, tiring hours on-set that were ahead of us.

The next morning, I went to the office pretty excited about this opportunity that had suddenly fallen into place so quickly. The first thing I did was head up the stairs to tell Harlan every detail of my itinerary. He was amazed at how fast it all came together. Then I went back downstairs and discussed it with Danny. He shook his head, made a face, humored me a little, and then pleaded with me to get back to work. We had worked together for a long time, and he knew how determined I could be, but we had a newspaper to build and a job to do, so he tried to keep me focused on that. I returned to my desk, but my mind was filled with visions of a *Rocky* experience in Las Vegas.

Each day, I would log onto BeInAMovie.com to see if they had updated the information. As I did more research, I began to suspect that the movie extras from this group would probably end up in the background rather than ringside since they were working for free. As it turned out, that was not necessarily true because many of the extras received plenty of camera time. But I was on higher mission to go the distance and was determined to secure a ringside seat. I needed to find out who was operating the set and who I could make a contact with. It was only October so I still had plenty of time to figure it all out. I was holding out for a better situation that would land me in the front row.

I kept the online search going at every chance, scouring the Internet for additional information on the production. Even though my reservation was approved to be an extra working for free, I wanted to get closer to the action and firmly believed something better was in store for me. I kept saying to myself, "Ringside, I want to be ringside, just like that guy in the picture."

Looking back, I realize that I had no inkling of the developments that were taking place in the universe on my behalf. This experience has taught me about the powerful effects of positive energy and the thought process regarding the Law of Attraction. Your everyday thoughts are manifested through your personal circle of influence. Most of everything you need in life is already there for you, waiting for you to discover it, including help from family, friends, connections, and, of course, a higher faith.

One night I was telling Danny about all the steps involved in my quest. Usually he would say that I was crazy or had a screw loose. He was always trying to get me back to work. But this time was different; he was paying attention to me as I thought out loud. That opened the door to talk some *Rocky* with him.

He shared a few insights about Las Vegas because his parents lived there, and he knew the town well. During our conversation, I had a sudden revelation. I remembered meeting his sister Sharon earlier that year at a Broadway play. She was a casting director for a popular cable TV channel in California. She had connections! Danny saw the signs of brilliance light up my face.

"What?" he asked.

"Your sister, Sharon, she's a casting director in California, right?"

"Yeah, so?"

"She has to know someone in the business who could get me closer to the action."

Danny looked at me with his usual expression of disdain and slowly shook his head. "No way."

"Oh, please, call your sister and ask if she could help me."

Danny kept saying no, and I kept begging. He used the excuse that it was too late to call her because it was after 9 p.m. I reminded him that she was on Pacific Time and was probably still at work.

"Call her, please." I pleaded and hounded until he finally picked up the phone.

He dialed her number, and I could hear the phone ringing on the speaker. My excitement was building; I was sure Sharon could help me secure that front row seat. She answered the phone and after a few seconds of small talk, I think she sensed he wanted to ask her something.

"What's up, Danny?"

"I was wondering if you could do me a favor. I have this guy at work who's a crazy *Rocky* fan." He explained my situation and asked her flat out if she could give me the name of a colleague on-set who could help me obtain a preferred seat. "Could you help him out?"

I held my breath as Sharon, who was on the speaker phone, quickly replied, "No, I'm not going to help this guy. He sounds cuckoo, and the last thing I need is for some nut trying to use my name around a set while he's causing trouble."

Her words deflated me like a popped balloon. She wiped the smile right off my face, but I'm a sales guy, and I don't take no for an answer. I quickly jumped up from my chair behind my desk and approached the speaker phone.

"Sharon, its Felice. I'm not cuckoo. I hope you remember that you met my wife and me in person a few months ago on Broadway. You saw that we were good people. I just want to be as close to the action as possible. Can you please help me?"

I went on to explain that working in the media business, I've been around hundreds of stars and famous folk of all kinds. I knew how to conduct myself around them. Sharon must have felt blindsided by my begging. She relented, but emphasized that she couldn't promise anything. She would make some calls to see if something could be done for me. My circle of influence was again working overtime. I thanked her and assured her that I wouldn't do anything on-set to embarrass her. When we hung up, I believed she would help. Danny just smiled and shook his head.

This phone call took place two weeks before I was scheduled to depart for Las Vegas. Every day, I would ask Danny if he had heard from his sister. When he said no, I would beg him to call her again, but he always refused.

"She will call us if she has any connections," he said. "Could you please just help me build a newspaper?"

Departure day was fast approaching, and I was still assigned to my original spot with a one-day reservation with BeInAMovie.com. I was scheduled to leave on Friday night, and I still hadn't heard back from Sharon. By that late date, I had just about given up; I didn't even bother to ask Danny about her anymore.

The afternoon of our flight, I was wrapping up my work early when my desk phone rang and the receptionist said Sharon was on the line. My sense of hope reignited, and I answered the phone confidently.

"Hi Sharon, thanks for getting back to me."

"Are you leaving for Vegas tomorrow?"

"No, tonight," I replied.

"Well, I'm sorry."

When she said those words, I knew it was not good news, and my excitement over the call evaporated. She explained that she had tried hard to find out if she knew anyone at Puncher Productions, the company that was handling the film. I was only half-listening to her, thinking that my plan was doomed. I would probably end up in the last row, far away from the action.

"The only thing I can tell you," she continued, "is that the company handling the paid extras is called Wild Streak. Here's what you should do. Tomorrow when you get to Vegas; give this girl Frankie a call, first thing in the morning."

She gave me Frankie's contact information and said I should tell her that I'm from New York and I am in town to be an extra with the other company. I should explain that I have some extra days available and ask if she needs any more help. Sharon reminded me that there were no guarantees, that it was the best she could come up with. She wished me good luck and a safe trip.

I thanked her and wrote down everything on the back of my business card, tucking it in my wallet for safe keeping. I was touched that Danny's sister had helped me out, and now the rest was up to me. After so many years of trying to make this happen, the key was finally in my back pocket. It would lead me to the next step of my journey toward personal fulfillment and success.

As I was leaving the office, I saw Danny and told him about my conversation with Sharon. He wished me a good time, with the hope that I would get it all out of my system so I could come back and be ready to work. Danny is tough when it comes to making money, but there is none better. If you did the job right, you were in good shape with this guy.

A million things went through my head as I headed home. I had no idea what life had in store for me. My family was packed, and we were out of the house on time. Our anticipation escalated as we looked forward to the visit with my mom, sister and her family in Las Vegas. We made a quick stop at Chrissy's parents' house to drop off our pet fish and get her dad to drive us to the JetBlue terminal at the Airport.

We were flying standby with our buddy passes, so it got a little tense as everyone else boarded the plane. We had to wait for the ticketed passengers to get on first, and then any available seats would be given in the order of check-in for standby passengers. The Law of Attraction was once again working in my favor as we got the first four vacant seats all together.

As we hit the sky, I knew that I was following my intention toward something significant. This Hollywood film would somehow connect to my physical world. My energy level soared as I continued to manifest an opportunity to achieve personal success and my future involvement in the *Rocky* franchise. I was ready to live the excitement of the adventure.

ROUND EIGHT

Ringside in Las Vegas

We landed exactly on time in Las Vegas, and when we deplaned, there was my brother-in-law Ed waiting to fly back to New York for business on the very same airplane. Our paths had crossed perfectly, and we said a quick hello and goodbye. My sister had just dropped him off and was waiting outside to pick us up. Everything continued to align itself.

My girls were so excited to be in Las Vegas, hanging out with their cousin, Aunt and Grandma. They weren't the least bit interested that I was going to see Rocky. That night we settled in at my sister's house. The plan was to wake up early Saturday morning and go out to breakfast. At 9 a.m., I had a cell phone appointment to call a girl named Frankie. Before falling asleep that night, I checked my wallet again to make sure her contact information was still there, and it was. All I could think about that night was the phone call.

We woke up early the next morning, appreciating the time-zone change. After breakfast, we went to the supermarket, and I clock-watched the entire time. We were in the parking lot loading the car with groceries when I noticed it was five minutes to nine. I stopped everyone and took the card from my wallet. I looked at my watch and waited for the exact stroke of 9 o'clock to dial Frankie's number.

I was nervous; this was my one shot, and truthfully, I didn't have a script prepared for the call. Being in sales gave me invaluable experience talking on the telephone, so in the end, I was ready. I dialed the number slowly to make sure I got it right. I waited for a pause and then heard a busy tone. My heart was racing; as I bought myself an extra minute. At 9:01, I dialed again, still busy. I told my wife and sister that we weren't going anywhere until I completed this call.

I waited until 9:05 and tried the number for a third time. It started to ring, once, twice, three times. A voice on the other end answered, "Hi this is Frankie." I gulped, and before I got a word out, she said, "Please hold."

That gave me a chance to collect my thoughts. I stood there waiting and thinking quickly about what I was going to say to her. A minute and a half later, she picked up and said in a hurried voice, "Hi, this is Frankie. How can I help you?"

She sounded busy, so in a fast, confident tone of voice I said, "Hi Frankie, my name is Felice Cantatore. A friend of mine, Sharon, who is a casting director, gave me your contact information. I live in New York, and I'm in Las Vegas to be an extra in *Rocky Balboa*. I'm scheduled to be on-set for one day, but I'm in Vegas until Wednesday, and I was calling to see if you had any extra days available."

"You're here in Vegas?"

"Yes."

"Are you available starting tomorrow?" she asked.

"Yes."

"Perfect timing," she said. "I just got a call from the production company. I was talking to them while you were on hold. They asked me for fifty more people for the next three days. Could you give me three days starting tomorrow?" Before I could answer, she said, "What do you look like"?

"Italian, I'm a big Italian guy, stereotypical Italian."

"Great, what are you wearing?" she asked.

"Excuse me?"

"On-set, what do you plan on wearing on-set?"

"Oh, a suit and tie." I laughed nervously. "I always wear a suit and a tie."

"Perfect."

What she said next were the most unbelievable words I'd ever heard and confirmed once again my belief in faith.

"We need people for the front row to be high rollers at the fight scene. What is your e-mail address?"

I was in shock. Chrissy and Angela tried to interpret the expression on my face as I kept hearing the words *front row, front row* in my head. Somehow I managed to give Frankie my e-mail address. She promised to send me the details and said she would see me the next morning at 6 a.m. Then she abruptly ended the conversation and hung up, just like that.

It was one of the most incredible moments of my life. I paused to collect my thoughts while my family stood there wondering what had just happened. Someone upstairs was definitely watching over me, and together, we had manifested one of my visions into a direct reality. I was really going to sit in the front row as a high-roller extra at the filming of *Rocky Balboa*—I was even going to be paid for it!

"What happened?" Chrissy asked.

Even though she tried to play it cool, she was pretty excited. She knew better than anyone what this moment meant to me. I never asked her, but I'm guessing she thought back to years earlier when I declared to someday be in the front row of a movie that didn't even exist yet. And now, here in some random supermarket parking lot in Las Vegas, it just became a reality. You can't make this stuff up. My universe was spinning in perfect alignment, and I was in total control. I was a magnet for the Law of Attraction.

Back in the car, I urged my sister to hurry home so I could check her computer for the e-mail. As soon as we returned to her house, I immediately logged on, and sure enough, there it was with an attachment filled with instructions and my assignment.

The e-mail started out by welcoming me to Wild Streak and the production of *Rocky Balboa*. Due to a marathon being run near the Mandalay Bay Hotel & Casino, it warned that there would be no parking available to us on Sunday, my first day. We were to meet up with a bus in the parking lot of a nearby gentlemen's club at 6 a.m. I read that curious statement a second time: The parking lot of a gentlemen's club at 6 a.m.—only in Vegas!

It detailed wardrobe options, suggesting that we wear on the bus what we planned to wear on-set and to bring an extra outfit in case we needed to make a wardrobe change. It requested that we not wear white shirts or red ties. I also stopped to read that line twice because the exact outfit I brought with me was a black suit, white shirt, and red tie. I started to panic because the other suit I brought also had a white shirt and a colorful bright tie. I'm a pretty big guy, and I have a hard time finding shirts in my neck size. What was I going to do now? My sister said not to worry, before we went out to dinner to celebrate her birthday, we could go shopping. Fortunately, her favorite restaurant was located inside the mall.

Later that afternoon, however, I began to fear that my luck had taken a wrong turn. I dashed from store to store, trying to find the right shirt and tie combination to go with my black suit. As I was running around under a great deal of pressure, my family waited outside of the entrance of the restaurant. Every five or ten minutes, my cell phone would ring. Angela reminded me that we had a reservation. I could hear my mother in the background complaining that she had to eat at a certain time, and where the heck was I, what was taking so long?

Talk about stress. My mom was grumbling, but I still had to find the perfect shirt and tie combination in my size, and I had to do it quickly. Finally, I stumbled into Dillard's Department Store and found a gold-colored shirt that matched a tie I had tossed into my luggage at the last minute, by chance, as an extra choice for no apparent reason at the time of packing. The shirt was one of the last in my size, and it was absolutely perfect. The extra tie now became the one that I eventually wore. I did manage to find a second shirt and tie to go with my alternate outfit.

I was back on a roll, but my euphoria only lasted for a few minutes as I ran back through the mall to meet my family. When I reached the restaurant, my mother gave me an earful about my tardiness. Chrissy wasn't too happy with me either, but she enjoyed seeing my Mom give me a piece of her mind. I tuned it out and didn't hear a word of her rant. I was back and ready for a great meal. My mind was focused only on what awaited me the next morning.

We had a nice dinner and celebrated Angela's birthday, but all I wanted to do was get back to her place and grab some sleep. I scheduled myself to wake up at 4 a.m. in order to be on time. I was so excited that it's a wonder how I ever fell asleep that night, not to mention the effects of the time-zone change that finally caught up with me.

Back at my sister's house, I ironed the two new shirts and finished packing my bag for the extra wardrobe change and our two nights at the Mandalay Bay. I went to sleep, and in what felt like an hour later, I was up showering and combing my Italian hairstyle into perfect shape. I was going Hollywood that day and I wanted to look the part.

After getting ready, I woke up my sister, and at 5 a.m. we were out the door, heading for a gentlemen's club in the heart of Las Vegas. I know this sounds a little corny, but leaving her house in the dark reminded me of the original *Rocky* training scene when he left his Philadelphia apartment for his morning run. I took a deep breath and watched the wisps of chilled air as I exhaled. I can't even tell you how great this moment was, and the feeling continued as we drove away. It was still dark and a little cold; the ride to this club was surreal. I was filled with anticipation and excitement, but my sister was tired, so we just small-talked as she drove. All I remember thinking is that it was Sunday morning at 5 a.m. and my sister was driving me to a gentlemen's club. I sat in the passenger seat and smiled to myself. This is what adventure and life are supposed to feel like, and it was an incredible rush.

We arrived at the parking lot at 5:30, and I assumed we were early, but we were not. The bus was all lit up, and people of every shape and size were standing in line, holding carry-on luggage. Angela pulled over and said this must be it. She wished me well, told me to enjoy myself, and to be careful.

"Do you have everything you need?" she asked.

"Yes." I thanked her for the ride and wished her luck watching my girls. "Isn't this cool?" I said.

She smiled and nodded yes. I knew she was happy to be a part of my adventure. It seems that certain people often share big moments in your life, and I was glad to be with Angela that morning.

As the sun was beginning to rise, I exited the car and looked back at her. She smiled again and waved, then waited to be sure I was in the right place. At that moment, everything seemed to be in the right place. I walked toward the bus in my perfectly pressed black suit, my new gold shirt and matching tie. My hair was absolutely flawless, not a strand out of place. It didn't even move with the gentle morning breeze. I took another deep breath as I approached the line by the bus. It was a strange scene to see everyone waiting to board, bundled up in coats and standing in line with their bags. No one was talking. It felt like I was heading off to boot camp.

I joined the back of the line and asked the person in front of me if this was the Wild Streak bus. He just nodded. It was like stepping into *The Twilight Zone*. I was really excited at this point, but played it cool because I didn't want to look like a rookie.

The line started moving and a nice young girl with a clipboard was checking names. I thought it might be Frankie. I was one of the last people to board the bus, and when I reached the door, I found out it was, indeed, her. I quickly introduced myself and thanked her for the opportunity. She gave me a once-over and said, "You really do look Italian."

I smiled and quietly entered the bus to wait for instructions. Frankie welcomed everyone and told us that when we arrived at the Mandalay Bay, we were to line up single file at the Wild Streak table to fill out our payroll paperwork. Then we would receive our assignments. Those selected as photographers or security guards should go to wardrobe for outfits and props. The rest should follow the high rollers into the arena and take a seat in the upper deck to wait for further instructions.

Again there was a weird silence, but maybe because it was still early. During the entire bus ride over and while we filled out our paperwork, no one said a single word to me. I was unsure of myself as to what I should be doing, so I paid attention and tried to follow everyone else. When I handed in my paperwork to Frankie, she again welcomed me and asked how long I would be in town.

"Until Wednesday."

"You can give me three days, right? I need three days out of you."

"Three days, definitely, count me in," I said. "You know my wife is available for tomorrow."

"What does she look like?" Frankie asked.

"Long, curly, blond hair and she's very pretty."

"Well, why don't you bring her here tomorrow? I could use more people for the next two days."

Wow! This was too good to be true; can you believe all these things that were happening to me? I signed Chrissy up for the next two days, along with three for myself, and handed in the paperwork. Then, with all the self-assurance in world, I strutted into the arena, just like I belonged.

This confidence only lasted for about twenty seconds. We arrived early, and the other agency didn't need us until 8 a.m. I thought we would have the entire arena to ourselves with our choice of seating; it would be just our little busload of high rollers. But as I walked inside, I was startled by the crowd already there. The place was packed with people sitting motionless in their seats. I felt a sense of disappointment come over me. *There goes my ringside seat*, I thought. *But how did so many people get here before me?* About a second later, I took a real good look at the motionless audience and quickly realized they were all dummies. The arena was packed with upper-torso mannequins dressed in wigs, hats, and shirts. It was an astonishing sight. Then I noticed a few stagehands moving around setting them up. The dummies were pretty funny-looking up close, but when I saw the finished product, the arena looked filled. An interesting side note is that every row had an empty seat or two for a real person to sit between the dummies to give the appearance of movement.

After figuring it out, I had to laugh at myself. We were the first group of extras to arrive, after all. I was smiling once again as my confidence level shot back up. I followed the others to the upper level to find a seat and drop off my bag. I stood by the railing and looked down at the ring. The place was already set up for a boxing match because the night before they had hosted an actual Las Vegas championship fight, which was a rematch between newly crowned Middleweight Champion Jermain Taylor and the man he defeated for the title, Bernard Hopkins.

The first day of filming took place with only a limited number of extras needed. On Saturday night during the real championship fight, they had used the live crowd for some authentic shots. They filmed Rocky's entrance scene as he was leaving the dressing room and heading for the ring.

I learned that the production company chose the Mandalay Bay to take advantage of having the arena already set up and the feel of an actual championship fight. Also, the HBO crew and familiar, big-fight faces would already be in town and available. The Taylor/Hopkins II fight promoter, Lou DiBella, a native New Yorker, worked his way into a movie role during some clever set negotiations, along with his unique attitude toward Stallone. I was quickly learning that the making of a motion picture, boxing, and the entertainment industry are definitely big business.

While we waited, I observed the set, quietly minding my own business, but maintaining a confident posture. I was surprised by the voice of someone speaking to me. A very nice older woman approached and asked who I was. She thought I looked important because I stood out from the others. Maybe she noticed my aura of confidence that I usually take on at game time, or maybe it was just my new gold shirt. Whatever, I was grateful that she broke the ice. Her name was Margo from Las Vegas, and she had been an extra in *Rocky IV*. She shared some of her movie experience and introduced me to her daughter, Adrian, who sat a few seats away from us. Her name, of course, made me smile as I thought about my own little girl. Margo was also a lifelong

Rocky fan, and her daughter's name was no accident. So another connection attracted two serious fans to each other. The friendly woman put me at ease and made me feel like I belonged. I've always wanted to thank her for that interaction.

Her daughter was also very nice, and later on when I got to talk to her, she gave me some background on some of our fellow extras, which helped me get acquainted. Many of them worked regularly with Wild Streak on different projects and were locals who knew each other. I guess I really did stand out as a true outsider.

While I was speaking to Margo, a young Asian girl was sizing me up. I noticed she was staring at me, and when I glanced at her, she asked, "Are you new? I haven't seen you at Wild Streak before."

I told her I was from New York and we started talking. Her name was Terri, and she seemed to know everyone on-set. She filled me in on what to expect that day and what to do with my bag. I could leave it in the upper level seats and not worry, nobody would take anything. She recognized me as the new guy and considered it her job to show me around. Terri turned out to be very helpful. We became instant friends, and by chance, I wound up sitting next to her for three whole days during the shoot.

"High rollers take your place. We need the high rollers."

One of the production assistants in charge of the extras called up to us, and everyone scrambled down to ringside to get the best seats. At first I wasn't sure what to do, but then it hit me that I better get down there quickly. I walked swiftly but carefully, to not run anyone over and embarrass myself. I was a little slow and ended up landing a third-row-center seat on the perfect side of the ring. It wasn't the front row, but I was pretty happy because the camera usually catches that side of the ring. I was dead center and marveled at my good luck. The production assistant shouted again, "Fill in the corners; fill in the corners. You, the big guy in the black suit, fill in over here."

She was talking to me; the production assistant had just moved me from third row middle to front row corner. Front row, does that sound familiar? Front row in a *Rocky* movie! An unbelievable feeling came over me. I was actually in the front row, very close to the same seat as that John Denver-looking guy in the photograph. This Law of Attraction stuff is serious.

I soon discovered that I was sitting next to my new friend, Terri. Then I began to hear some commotion going on behind me and stood up to look. An entourage was heading down the aisle with former Heavyweight Champion Mike Tyson. As he passed by me, I got to pat him on the back. He eventually sat down in the front row, center, which would have placed him directly in front of me if I had stayed in my original seat. I was now feeling bummed about my move. But then I noticed that I was sitting right next to the entranceway where the fighters come in. This would be a great seat after all. I should definitely get some camera time when the fighters entered or left the ring. I felt my thoughts shift back to positive thinking because here I was in the front row, ringside for a Rocky Balboa fight. It doesn't get much better than this.

I settled into my seat next to Terri and felt lucky because she knew everyone. It didn't take me long to get comfortable. It was as if I'd known the people around me for awhile. In reality, we had just met and all seemed like-minded.

As I was getting acquainted with some of the other extras sitting around us, things started to happen fast. Familiar faces emerged from the fighters' entrance and popped up right next to me. It was a gaggle of famous people, such as Frank Stallone, Tony Burton (Rocky's manager), Michael Buffer (the let's-get-ready-to rumble guy), Jim Lampley, Larry Merchant and Max Kellerman (HBO commentators), real-life boxing champion Antonio Tarver (current Rocky opponent Mason "The Line" Dixon) and Pedro Lovell (who played Spider Rico). Seconds later came the moment I will always remember. There he was, wearing black and yellow boxing shorts and a sleeveless jacket: Rocky Balboa—I mean Sylvester Stallone—no, I mean Rocky Balboa! To me they are two different guys, and I bet if you asked Sly himself, he would agree, even though their stories of motivation and success are similar.

In a rush of jumbled impressions, I thought, he's not really all that short; he's average height. He does look a little older, but he's in incredible shape for a fifty-nine year-old man. The one person in the world (and his alter ego) that I always wanted to meet was standing right there before my eyes. It was surreal. All of my efforts had paid off as I manifested this truly great Hollywood moment into my life.

I sat there, quietly taking in all the excitement and playing it cool. As I mentioned before, I've been around famous people throughout my media career, and like I told Danny's sister, the casting director, I knew how to handle myself. I was calm until I saw Burt Young. My plan was to revisit our meeting at the diner from many years past. The second I saw him, I didn't hesitate and quickly waved at him. Burt acknowledged me with a wave back and a smile. He was close enough for me to shout over to him, which I did. I mentioned that I was from the old neighborhood, and he smiled again. As he was turning away, I called out the name of my godfather and the old carpet company. That caught his attention, and this time he walked over to give me a hug and ask a few questions about myself and what I was doing there. I will never forget that hug from Burt, as it was another great connection to this man who was a huge presence in the *Rocky* universe. You have to love this guy; Burt Young and his character Paulie are both legends.

Burt kept smiling at me and then yelled over to his nephew in the next section, relating that I was from the old neighborhood. He confirmed that he knew my godfather, which gave credence again to a favorite family story.

For the next three days Burt treated me like an old friend. He stopped by my seat many times to pat me on the back and ask how I was doing. It was awesome getting this attention from one of the only stars who appeared in every *Rocky* movie ever made. Some of the other extras told me they wondered who I was because of his interest in me. The interactions with him made me feel like I belonged and was in the movie business forever. Everything was falling into place.

The production crew was on a tight schedule, and they certainly wasted no time at all. Most of the fight scenes were shot out of sequence, with action happening all over the ring. The actors were working hard and so was the entire crew. I use the word amazing often to describe my experience, but it was amazing to watch so many people locked into their jobs, all taking direction from Sylvester Stallone.

It was interesting to see how the makeup artist applied authentic looking bruises and swelling between takes. They sprayed the actors with bottles filled with what appeared to be water to make them look sweaty. I give Stallone a lot of credit. He worked hard, both acting and directing, and was all business most of the time. He even exchanged some real punches with Tarver during the filming. He explained to everyone within listening distance that he wanted to make this film as realistic as possible. At one point, I overheard him say that with the advantage of high-definition cameras and the flexibility of camera angles, this movie would change the way the sport of boxing would be covered in the future. He also knew this might be his last *Rocky* movie, and he seemed sentimental about soaking it all in. After all, the character of Rocky Balboa was developed through his own personal manifestation and has been a part of him for more than thirty years. I wondered again what was going through his mind.

Our job as extras was to get into the spirit of the fight and cheer appropriately at the action, both good and bad. Our main responsibility was to shout the Rocky chant when cued. We spent hours swinging our fists and chanting in unison, "Rocky! Rocky! Rocky!" Other times, we just mouthed the words when the stagehand called out for us to pantomime, meaning that she wanted action, but no sound.

One time, they asked a few of us to cheer for Mason Dixon as he connected with a few jabs. Being clearly in Rocky's corner, I refused to do that. I was only going to root for one guy, and that is exactly what I did.

After fourteen hours on-set that day, my voice was shot at the end, but it didn't matter; the whole experience had been tremendous. Being involved in the filming of this movie was one of the coolest things I ever accomplished. I really got into it during the action. I was anxious when Rocky took hits, and cheered out of control when he was the one landing punches. We all got a good laugh after one particular exchange between the fighters. As Rocky (Stallone) delivered a few shots at Dixon (Tarver), almost by instinct, Tarver, the professional boxer-turned-actor, fired back a real jab with lightning speed to Stallone's jaw.

"Hey, you're not supposed to hit me," Stallone retorted.

He rubbed his chin in pain and moved his jaw from side to side as he played to the crowd. We all realized by now that they were throwing real punches, and Stallone showed his commitment to authenticity with a good sense of humor. After seeing that Sly could take a real punch, I went back to cheering for my guy. If I was going to be on camera, then I wanted to excel at playing the part I was hired for.

Some great action erupted in our corner, and I tried to position myself to be filmed supporting Rocky. After the scene, I noticed Stallone putting on his robe. They removed some of his cosmetic bruises, and I wondered if they were going to shoot his entrance to the ring. As they moved toward the dressing room, it was confirmed. I was charged up knowing that Rocky would walk right past my seat. I never dreamed that something like this would happen. When he passed in front of me on his way to the ring, I was stunned. I have no idea what my reaction was and may have patted him on the back. This was exciting because surely the entrance scene had to be in the movie.

I thought: This couldn't possibly get any better. But it could, and it did. Moments later, they needed people to sit behind the HBO announcers as they filmed their commentary scene. They picked our section to fill in and positioned me directly behind them. My face was right between Lampley and Merchant, who were sitting next to Kellerman. A photograph of Stallone and the HBO announcers with me in it was featured on the authorized *Rocky* Web site. The photo bears an official MGM trademark and is on proud display in my office.

The day was already half over, so we broke for lunch. I was destined to spend fourteen exhausting hours on-set that day, but my adrenaline was pumping. After all, this was a *Rocky* dream come true, and I didn't want it to end.

I learned a quick lesson about the difference between union and nonunion extras like me. Members of the Screen Actors Guild (SAG) ate first and were served hot food. We nonunion people received a generic bagged lunch consisting of a turkey sandwich, chips, a mint and a bottle of water. I grabbed my lunch and managed to sit next to the famous ring announcer Michael Buffer. I had a brief conversation with him, always being careful not to go overboard. I also networked myself a little to set up for the following day, as I thought ahead to plan my next moves.

The rest of this first day was very busy. We chanted our hearts out with the swinging-fist, *Rocky* mantra. I did whatever I could to get myself into more scenes again, but mindful of staying within my cautious limits. By the end of the day, I could feel the effect of the many hours on-set, plus the additional time to drive there. But I was equal to the task, and it was certainly worth the effort.

That evening, Chrissy met up with me and we stayed at the Mandalay Bay Hotel. In spite of my fatigue, we shared a pleasant dinner and I filled her in on what to expect on her first day. After our meal, I noticed a row of Rocky-themed slot machines outside the restaurant. Naturally, I couldn't resist playing them, and we wound up donating a few dollars to Las Vegas. We had some fun with those one-armed bandits, which added to our overall experience. After losing some coins, we called it quits and headed up to our room to prepare for the next day's adventure. Our decision to stay in the hotel had been a good idea.

We got up early the next morning and were ready to head down to the arena at 6 a.m. It was an easy walk from our room. I was now a one-day veteran on-set, so I signed us in and helped Chrissy with her paperwork. The extras were shouting for everyone to sit in the same seats for the sake of continuity to make it look like the scenes were all shot on the same day. We had been instructed to wear the exact same clothing as the day before. I wore my black suit, gold shirt and tie for three consecutive days. When we got down to the seats, I looked around and found Chrissy a good spot about three rows behind me.

The second day on-set was also tremendous, as they shot scenes in the corner of the ring, right where we were sitting. During some major action shots, I again tried to position my head in the picture. Along with the crowd, I was super animated, especially during one knockdown that happened in our corner. I figured that scene stood a good chance to be in the movie.

It was an exciting day, from start to finish. My wife was moved into a crowd shot at one point, and she met some strange and interesting people sitting around her. We still have a good laugh when we see them in the actual movie on DVD. The entire day's experience was long and a bit overwhelming for her, but I was happy that she joined me and saw the production for herself.

The highlight of day two happened during a scene being shot of fight promoter Lou DiBella sitting among the extras. Stallone, who was also directing the production, stopped to kneel and angle the shot. I was sitting in the front row corner, and here he was, only a foot away. *Holy cow*, I thought to myself, *Rocky Balboa was kneeling directly in front of me*. I've been watching this character for thirty years, and now I could reach out and touch him if I wanted to. When the scene broke, I must have made ten cell phone calls to my friends back home to share yet another moment that I will never forget.

We spent fourteen more hours on-set that day, but I was in my element and loved every minute of it. At lunch and during the downtime, I talked to a few more people involved in the production. I enjoyed asking a few questions of Milo Ventimiglia, the actor who played Rocky's son in the movie, and to say a few words to Frank Stallone, another guy I was thrilled to meet. Frank videotaped almost everything that went on and was one of the nicest guys on-set. He found time to interact with everybody and was very popular with the extras. I also got to see Burt a few more times and introduced him to my wife. Speaking of Chrissy, the long day was tough on her because we sat apart most of the time. She decided to let me go alone on the third and final day, knowing it would be crazy and I would probably be in my own world.

When the second day was over, we went to an upscale restaurant in the hotel where we celebrated our eighth wedding anniversary with a romantic dinner. It was the perfect scenario. We were feeling wonderful, and I couldn't have planned it any better.

The next day, they were shooting the end of the movie, and it was an important segment for the production. They needed lots of extra people to fill up the arena and give the impression the place was packed during the big final scene. The crew wound up grabbing people at random from the hotel to sit in the audience. Stallone was in a joyous mood as he told us in a heartfelt speech what the movie meant to him and clarified the moral behind the story. He explained that age is just a number. It has no capability to prevent you from achieving your dreams. As long as your mind can focus on a goal, you can accomplish anything—a sentiment I share with him. As Rocky the character aged, so did Stallone the actor. The movie was meant to show the world that anything is possible, both in the arts and in the spirit of real life.

For Stallone, the filming of *Rocky Balboa* proved that life does move forward, and it's up to you to write your own script. In choosing to proceed with this sequel, Stallone lived out the moral of the movie. Once again, the life stories of the actor and Rocky paralleled each other. I'm so glad that I chose to move forward along with them.

After explaining his motivation to write and direct the movie, Stallone thanked us all for being a part of it. It felt like we had formed a bond with this man. He then did something surprising. He gave us permission to take photographs on-set. This is typically not allowed, but since it was the sixth installment of this amazing franchise, I think he wanted us to take home some great memories. We appreciated this gesture, as Sly certainly went out of his way to include us in this wonderful experience.

On this day, they shot the scene where everyone jumps into the ring at the end of the big fight, and it was over-the-top exciting. They did several takes and each time I was able to run up and pound on the floor of the boxing ring. One time, I jumped forward so fast that I almost took out one of the actors playing a fight judge. It makes me laugh each time I see the fellow with the white hair rush into the ring on DVD because I nearly flattened the poor guy.

I was surprised to be able to gain such access to the ring during this scene. I probably could have gotten away with jumping in, or at least standing on the apron, which would have been very cool. I considered it for a second, but was smart enough not to take the chance of annoying anyone or doing the wrong thing. Every second of production costs a lot of money, and the last thing I wanted was to stick my nose where it certainly didn't belong. Maybe the warning from Danny's sister to behave myself was still in my head.

Being in this scene stands out as one of the many incredible highlights of my three-day adventure. Every time Rocky Balboa exited the ring on three separate takes, I was standing next to him as he walked down the ringside steps. It felt like I was personally escorting him as he headed back to the dressing room.

Stallone shot several versions of the ending that day, with different final outcomes of the fight. Right before filming one of the endings, he again grabbed the microphone to address the crowd. He told us he wanted to go out in style and that we should give it everything we had on this take. "Don't hold back," he said. "Go crazy."

That's all I needed to hear and went absolutely nuts. As Rocky was leaving the apron on this one particular take, he turned back to face the ring. I shoved an extra actor playing a security guard out of the way really hard. Then I grabbed Rocky's arm and raised it in victory! For me, this was the Holy Grail of *Rocky* moments, one that I will never, ever forget; it took unbelievable determination. I, Felice Cantatore, was raising the arm, not of the actor, but of Rocky Balboa, one of my favorite movie characters in the world. It was as surreal as surreal could ever be.

My two worlds collided in that moment. I felt like a character in the movie, as if it were my real life. Was it real? I must admit, it sure felt like it. I figured it would end up on the DVD in the extra-scenes section because it was an alternate ending. But it wasn't an alternate ending for me, it was the ultimate experience. I was flying sky-high full of boundless energy. I sure would love to find a picture of that one scene someday.

After that experience, I felt suffused with the Rocky Spirit. It was my last day on-set. My time was winding down, but I had one more encore act. During a break in the action, Frank Stallone was taking home videos to document the production for his brother. I stopped to speak to him and had a nice conversation. I even introduced him to some of the people hanging around as if he were my lifelong friend. While Frank was visiting with some extras in the crowd, I suggested that he give me his video camera so I could film him conversing with them, and he agreed.

I took the camera and filmed for a few minutes, narrating as I went along. I knew this footage would become a part of the Stallone family archives and was honored that Frank allowed me to work his camera. When finished, I turned it around and introduced myself on film to the Stallone family, thanking them for including me in this grand event. I still wonder if they ever watched that footage and asked, "Who is that guy?"

The day ended with me talking to some of the actors and meeting more of the extras. I succeeded in accomplishing my goals onset by doing what I dreamed about for many years. The one thing I didn't do, though, was bother Sly. I said a few words to him in passing, but never introduced myself, except of course in the video. At the end of the production day, I wanted to go over and thank him, but one of the real-life security guards from the hotel was taking his job a little too seriously and blocked my access. So I left it alone, as if I knew there would be another chance to meet him one of these days.

That was a wrap of my three days on-set. There were two more scheduled days of production left, and Frankie asked me to stay, but knew I had to get back to work. I had called Danny to test the idea of changing my plans, and he suggested that I stay the extra days, which was most unusual for him. The universe really was working in my favor, but I had to get my girls back to school, too. When I learned that most of the crowd shots had been completed, and the next two days would not be all that busy, I decided to go home as planned. During the entire flight, however, I kept second-guessing whether I should have stayed.

I couldn't wait to share my experience with anyone who would listen, but I also suffered excitement-withdrawal symptoms. Those three days on-set would be hard to match. I felt a void when I returned to work and my real-life routine. I could never have imagined how much *Rocky* excitement would continue to come my way. In fact, the following year would prove to be all about the film, in anticipation of the release of *Rocky Balboa*.

The Law of Attraction continued to manifest. I thought about my *Rocky* experience and the things that kept connecting me to the movie, believing that there was more to come. I became strong minded and locked in; the next year would prove to be a roller coaster of excitement.

ROUND NINE

Next Steps

A few days after returning home, an early Christmas present arrived in the mail. Three checks for each day I was on the set were sent to me from Puncher Productions. Each one was for a little more than a hundred dollars gross and around ninety dollars after taxes. "Your employer is Puncher Productions *Rocky VI*" was printed on the front of the envelopes. They were addressed to me, although the spelling of my last name was off by one letter. That upset me at first, but I thought back to the original *Rocky* when his boxing shorts were presented in the wrong color on the giant poster at ringside. The fight promoter, Miles Jergens, told him that it didn't matter, but Rocky eventually made it matter, and I felt the same way.

I opened the first two envelopes to photocopy and scan the checks, pay stubs and the envelope itself. I cashed the first two, but when the third one came, I decided to keep it, still sealed in its envelope. I figured I'd probably never find anything as cool as that to add to my collection for the mere hundred dollars printed on its face. So it remains part of my *Rocky* memorabilia collection, stored away as one of the all-time, great souvenirs. Chrissy wasn't as sentimental and didn't think twice about cashing her check right away.

Speaking of the mail, right around Christmas time, I received a card from Margo, the first woman I met on-set. She sent photos from the production, obviously knowing how much I would appreciate them. I was surprised and happy to receive the package. It just shows how you can make an easy connection with certain people, especially when you share a wavelength. I met some wonderful extras on-set. I stayed in touch with some of them through e-mail when I returned from my adventure to perpetuate the excitement of the experience.

In Vegas, I had spoken to Burt Young about their plans for filming the rest of the production in Philadelphia. He said they were going to start in January and would be there for a while. As soon as I returned home, I began researching online about the Philly shoot. I found the name of the casting agency and was eager to pursue it, but I finally came to my senses. It was time to get back to work. Deep down, I realized I'd had my experience, and didn't want to detract from the great Vegas days. I guess it's about knowing your limits.

I still kept my eyes on what was going on by using the Google alerts feature online. I read everything I could find about *Rocky Balboa*, leading up to its intended release in December 2006. I couldn't wait to see if I had made the final cut of the movie. As an extra, there are no guarantees.

Midway through the year, I heard there would be a premiere showing of the film in Philadelphia in December. This news gave me a brand new *Rocky* goal to focus on. I simply had to attend the premiere of *Rocky Balboa*. It was too close for me not to go. The fact that I didn't pursue the filming over the winter, along with my old mistake of passing on the 20th anniversary party, probably fueled the desire to make this my new mission. It seemed that every setback gave me a push forward.

As August rolled around, my *Rocky* fever was blazing hot. I was consumed by thoughts of the December release, still wondering if I had made the final cut and buying *Rocky* items like crazy on eBay. I conveniently planned this little family vacation that included my old friend Pete and his family. We would spend a day at Hershey Park again, sandwiched between two days of exploring tourist attractions in Philadelphia. I researched the location of movie sites such as Mighty Mick's Gym, which had become a dollar store, and Rocky's apartment, along with another trip to the Rocky Steps. On TotalRocky.com, I found most of the addresses and started to MapQuest the itinerary.

Pete and I were excited about Philly, but the girls and kids were only interested in Hershey Park; at least they were willing to tag along. Our trip turned out to be a lot of fun. We saw all the great sites from the first five films and a few new ones, such as the restaurant that Rocky owned in the upcoming movie. We became familiar with the streets of Fishtown as we drove around for several hours trying to find Rocky's apartment and Paulie's house. We saw how tough life is for the people who live in some of the poverty-stricken neighborhoods.

The highlight of our excursion was cruising down those old, familiar Philadelphia streets. When Pete and I took a photograph together in front of Rocky's apartment at 1818 Tusculum Street, it was like being in our own little world. After seeing all the famous locations, we returned for another visit to the Rocky Steps at the Philadelphia Museum of Art. There is something compelling about those steps that brings out the energy of the Rocky Spirit in all of us, including our wives and children, who surprisingly jumped around with their arms raised in victory when they reached the top step and posed for photos. We took a lot of pictures of what felt like our home away from home.

It was amazing how one situation led to another during my year-long *Rocky* adventure. Whenever I accomplished a goal related to my quest, it somehow led to my next idea. I always seemed to be in the right place at the right time. I might have done something for one reason and then benefited later on in an unpredictable manner. Was it divine intervention that followed me, or more likely, spiritually leading the way?

One thing that kept happening throughout the year was that everyone who knew me was aware of my fascination with the *Rocky* movies. So whenever friends saw something about them online, they would point it out to me. If any of the movies were shown on television, they would tell me they had watched it. If Rocky was mentioned in the newspaper or a magazine, I was told about it. Maybe they were feeding off my own personal energy. Even those who liked to make fun of my passion would discuss *Rocky* with me when it came up in conversation. I was attracting everything *Rocky* into my world.

One on the best examples of attracting certain things came shortly after I returned from our trip to Philadelphia. An interesting book titled *Rocky Stories: Tales of Love, Hope, and Happiness at America's Most Famous Steps* turned up on my desk, given to me by our *Press* Editor-in-Chief. The book was written by Pulitzer Prize-winning journalist Michael Vitez and award-winning photographer Tom Gralish, with a foreword by Sylvester Stallone. Both authors were newspaper men working for the *Philadelphia Inquirer*. I excitedly paged through the book and saw that it examines the unique concept of what motivates people from around the world to run the famous Rocky Steps. The timing of receiving this book was unbelievable, coming as it did right after we had run the very same steps ourselves. Our editor had received a complimentary copy from the publisher because they were looking for some coverage in local newspapers. They were timing its publication with the release of the new movie. In some cosmic way, they definitely sent this book to the right person. After paging through a few stories, I asked our editor if I could write a mini-review in the *Long Island Press* for our book-of-the-week column. He approved of my suggestion and I quickly sent an e-mail to both Vitez and Gralish.

They answered me within minutes, thanking me for my interest. I let them know that not only was I an extra in the filming of *Rocky Balboa,* but my family had just run the steps two weeks earlier. I included a photograph of us as proof. In the picture, you could see the renovation work being done on the George Washington statue, and this confirmed that it was a current photograph.

We agreed by e-mail to talk on the telephone, and when Vitez and I connected, the discussion focused on the *Rocky* franchise, and of course, his book. Michael and Tom became great networking contacts for me. These guys had just written a book that was endorsed by Stallone, and they also worked in the newspaper industry. We were sharing a wavelength through the Law of Attraction.

As I read the book in preparation for my review, I came across some interesting stories about people from around the world who considered their trek up those steps to be an important part of their life's journey. I was inspired by those who overcame obstacles, such as illness. The goal of reaching the top and raising their arms in victory symbolized their success. I enjoy running those steps because of the energy it produces, and the book confirmed I was not alone. The fact that millions have shared this same vibrating energy is a powerful notion.

In reading the individual stories, I became intrigued by one guy who dressed like Rocky in the famous, grey sweatsuit. He earned a few bucks doing an impersonation of the Southpaw from Philly and having his picture taken with other visitors. The guy didn't look much like Rocky, but he had the outfit down to perfection, including the light blue towel around his neck. This story sparked some creative ideas, the first one being that the sweatsuit would be the perfect Halloween costume for me. The other thought worked its way into my head and manifested as my next journey.

In the middle of August, I started dropping hints about the upcoming premiere in Philadelphia with Danny. I revealed that my new mission was to attend the gala screening and the celebrity after-party. Since Danny and I ran a local newspaper and handled advertising for most of the movie companies, I asked him if he could once again help me by obtaining an invitation using our contacts. He said I should put on my promotional thinking cap, and if I came up with a successful marketing proposal for the release of the movie, he would help me.

"Don't worry," he said. "We'll get you there, even though you're out of your mind."

He always had to throw that in when talking to me about Rocky, but he did promise he'd do his best to get me an invite.

By late August, I was still trying to come up with the great idea. It had to be big, so this assignment was a tough one. I discussed some possible scenarios with Danny, but nothing seemed to click. My thoughts centered on that premiere and after-party; I wanted to rekindle some of those Vegas experiences. I continued to search for information on the Internet for something that would jumpstart my creativity. One day I received a Google alert about the rededication of the famous, bronze Rocky statue during a special promotional event called "Philly Week" that was coming up in September.

The main component of this event would take place at the Philadelphia Museum of Art. The city was planning a statue-rededication ceremony along with an outdoor showing of the original *Rocky* film on a large, portable screen in front of the museum steps. They would also hold a media press conference with Sylvester Stallone himself to promote the release of *Rocky Balboa*. My Philadelphia newspaper friends didn't know it yet, but they were about to assist me with my next great opportunity.

My concentration now shifted from the premiere to this statue rededication event. I had to be part of it, especially since it was a press conference, and after all, I was the press. The Law of Attraction struck again as one adventure led to the next. Once I learned all the details of the event, I started to formulate my action plan. Since it was going to be a press conference, I could use my media connections to make things happen, in particular, my friends at the *Philadelphia Inquirer* who provided me contact information for the people handling the festivities.

In regards to the *Long Island Press*, I enjoyed taking photographs for the publication and often attended certain events just to capture that one special image. So I reasoned that I should cover this event in Philly to get a photograph of Stallone that we could feature in our newspaper. I also figured that since it was such a big event, I would need two assistants, my childhood buddies Pete and Joe, to come along with me. Whenever possible, I tried to include these guys in my adventures. Like Rocky's friendship with Paulie, these guys always came along for the ride, especially when it was Rocky-related, because we all grew up with these movies—and they get it.

I found the organization in charge by contacting the Greater Philadelphia Film office and using my *Long Island Press* e-mail address to express my interest in covering the event. By the end of the day, I received a reply thanking me for my interest and asking if I needed anything regarding it. I guess my energy was taking control at this point because it couldn't have been easier. Every time I took on a new goal related to my journey, things just fell into place.

I quickly responded to confirm that I would be attending, along with my two assistants, Pete and Joe. They followed up stating that we were all welcome and they would forward a complete itinerary with the times and locations, including press access and parking availability at the very top of the Rocky Steps. I never realized you could park your car just past the top of them. This access gave us an opportunity to be situated right next to Stallone, the guest of honor, the moment he arrived.

Only a few weeks earlier, I had driven my family crazy as we cruised nearly every street in Philadelphia. We checked out each *Rocky* movie site, so now I knew my way around most of the city and was ready for this journey.

I left work early that Friday afternoon. Pete took the whole day off, and Joe took a half day off from his job. To make things go smoothly, Pete met me in the *Press* parking lot. We drove my car into the city to pick up Joe and then through the tunnel for an easy ride to Philadelphia. As three childhood friends skipped out on a workday to head to Philly, we felt like players in another movie called *City Slickers*. We were downright giddy about our adventure. It was going to be a special day because we were all lifelong fans and this was a chance to visit the famous steps again, see the statue, and meet Stallone in person.

The drive to Philadelphia was quick and we executed the trip exactly as planned, one of the few times that all three of us were on time. I had the itinerary and necessary contacts to ensure that we got to the event without any problems. The plan was for us to arrive around 4 p.m. to be on top of the steps for the photo opportunity, then down below for the statue dedication, and finally over to the press conference. Afterward, we planned to finish our night at the now-famous Victor Café for a late-night dinner. It was used in the upcoming *Rocky Balboa* movie doubling as Adrian's Restaurant, which was owned by Rocky.

We found the reserved parking for the press right next to the museum. Being early, we had some extra time on our hands so the three of us took photographs of ourselves, and never looked better. We hadn't been this excited about an adventure in a long time. We were content to be there, and it showed on our faces. I knew the three of us were sharing the same thoughts about the anticipation of seeing Stallone in person. It was a fraternal bond; we related our early years to the *Rocky* movie, the character, and the actor. Here we were, standing at this legendary location, and we felt at home. It's a special place filled with energy.

As we waited at the top of the steps for the event to begin, the excitement mounted; something big was about to happen. There were media outlets everywhere and plenty of photographers, including the three of us from the *Long Island Press*.

Suddenly, police officers started clearing the walkway behind the steps as a patrol car escorted a shiny, black Mercedes Benz driving through. The car was driven by Jimmy Binns, Stallone's lawyer and friend, who played two different roles in *Rocky V* and *Rocky Balboa*. Mr. Binns was responsible for working with the mayor of Philadelphia, the Honorable John F. Street, and the museum board of directors, to allow the famous Rocky statue to be permanently placed at the bottom right of the museum steps.

The statue placement had received opposition from some of the board members because they felt it was not an actual work of art and therefore didn't deserve a permanent spot in front of the museum. *Rocky* fans from around the world felt differently, of course, and thanks to the efforts of Mayor Street and Mr. Binns, the glorious, bronze statue now resides where it belongs. The mayor pointed out that the statue symbolizes what Rocky and Sylvester Stallone mean to the city of Philadelphia. It was a way for the people to thank the character, and especially the actor, for their continuous generosity to the city.

As the black Mercedes came to a stop and the doors slowly opened, I first saw Mr. Binns. I easily recognized him because of his finely groomed white hair, and he looked exactly as he did in *Rocky V*. The next person out of the car was Frank Stallone holding a video camera, probably the same one he used at the Vegas shoot. I smiled and remembered using that camera myself back then. I was happy to see Frank because he is friendly and approachable. I intended to talk to him and believed he would remember me.

We waited a long minute until the passenger-side door finally opened and Sly slowly emerged from the vehicle to the roar of a crowd gathered at the bottom of the steps. The media began to stir as he appeared, dressed in casual blue jeans and a black sports coat. He waved to everyone as cameras snapped away, including ours. Sly then walked over and struck the famous Rocky pose with two arms raised toward the sky. We all captured this unique picture. What made it so unusual was that we have seen Rocky Balboa on top of the steps before, but this time it was actually Sylvester Stallone not in character.

He made his way down the side of the steps to the podium where the *Rocky III* statue remained covered, awaiting its rededication. It reminded us of the actual scene in the movie back in the Eighties, and now here we were, living it and loving it. We descended straight down the steps through the massive crowd and over to the press area next to the podium. I found the contact who made our arrangements, and she ushered us into the press area with no problem. The three of us felt important. I can't say for sure, but I think she was excited to have the event covered by someone from the New York media.

The speeches began with Mr. Binns taking the lead, and we were in a perfect location to take additional photographs and a video. An unfortunate incident happened when Mayor Street was introduced to the Philadelphia crowd. The people from the City of Brotherly Love greeted their mayor with a round of boos. I felt sorry for him and cheered loudly from the side of the stage; after all, he did work hard to get the Rocky statue permanently placed in the spot where it rightfully belongs. I acted as if he was my guy, even though I didn't know anything about his politics. I had to chuckle when he looked right at me, smiled and nodded, as if to say thank you for the support. Two people standing next to me thought I worked for the mayor's office, probably because I was cheering so loudly, and I was one of only a few people wearing a suit and tie. I felt it couldn't hurt to position myself in a good spot with the mayor, especially when it came to the upcoming press conference, as I continued to look for my edge.

The ceremony moved forward, and when Sly took his turn at the podium, the three of us listened intently to his every word. He began with a classic "Yo, Philly!" and immediately connected to the audience. We continued to take photographs and wound up getting some excellent video footage. It was another cool experience to be up close at this event. After Sly's speech, and as he stirred up the crowd, the cord was pulled to remove the black cover and reveal the famous bronze statue in its now-permanent home. People were applauding loudly as this is what we all came to see. Stallone showed sentimental appreciation as he glanced up at his own likeness, and the giant statue cast a large shadow over him.

Afterward, we quickly moved behind the stage where important people had gathered. We ran into Frank as we were snapping pictures of ourselves near the statue. I walked up to say hello, and he looked as if he recognized me, but was not sure. I reintroduced myself and reminded him that we met on-set in Las Vegas. I was the guy that worked his camera and introduced him to some of the other extras. I was sure he would remember me. Pete and Joe were impressed by this interaction as they knew what I was up to. I'm pretty good at laying the groundwork that could potentially help any part of my next move. This technique increased my chances of attracting the necessary connections to help reach my goals. Networking was a specialty of mine and it also was a good idea to have Frank on our side at the press conference.

After a few more photographs, we followed the rest of the media to a restaurant and lounge called Water Works behind the museum where we checked in again without any problems. The place was impressive, and the press conference was conducted waterside in an outdoor area next to the scenic Schuylkill River.

We entered the restaurant lobby and looked around. It only took about two minutes before we spotted Stallone up close once again. Pete and Joe understood the main task of the night; their mission was to get a photograph of Sly and me together. Being in the media business, I rarely bother celebrities for photographs, and especially autographs. I learned that lesson early in my career when I was a twenty-one year-old intern with NBC Sports. I almost lost my internship when I met Joe DiMaggio at Old Timer's Day back in 1986 while working with the production team. I asked for and received his autograph, only to be scolded seconds later by a cranky Yankee executive who complained to the head of NBC Sports. I was warned that if I wanted to stay in the media business, I should never do that again. His valid advice has stayed with me throughout the years of my career, and I try to be circumspect around celebrities. There is certainly a difference between working in the media business and being a fan of something or someone. On this night, however, I was a fan, and the plan was for Pete or Joe to snap my picture with Sylvester Stallone.

We never expected it to be easy, but we couldn't possibly have imagined how perfect the opportunity would come about. As we entered the lobby of the restaurant, we literally ran into him. He was larger than life, standing right there in front of us. It must have been hilarious to see the expression on our faces at that moment. Here we were, three grown men, but we instantly became kids all over again, face to face with the man who invented Rocky. I wasted no time in accomplishing our mission. I approached him just as his security team attempted to escort him to the press conference podium. I quickly asked him for the photo opportunity, and he stopped, turned around, and posed with me on the spot. I placed my arm around his shoulder and smiled like I was a long-lost friend as Joe snapped the picture. It was an epic moment for me.

The security team again tried to usher Stallone away, but I introduced myself and said I was an extra at the Las Vegas shoot. He stopped and gave me this curious look, like I was familiar to him. His strange expression made me wonder if he remembered me as the guy who raised his arm during filming of the fight. I assume that he must have watched that scene a few hundred times and recognized me from that, or maybe even from the home video on his brother's camera. I often think about that time when I raised Rocky Balboa's arm in victory. That scene never did appear anywhere, but it will always live on in my memory. How many people actually get the opportunity to enjoy that type of interaction with their favorite movie character? I will always wonder why Stallone looked back at me with such a curious expression that night. I believe it was for a reason, or possibly a future connection that still might come my way.

When the security team finally led the guest of honor away, we followed him into an outdoor lounge area that was set up for the press conference. To our delight, the podium was surrounded by the brand-new poster for the release of *Rocky Balboa,* which was scheduled around Christmas time. It featured Rocky on the steps, not in his traditional stance with two arms raised in victory, but this time with just one arm stretched up high into the sky. That one-armed pose quickly registered in my mind. I took a photograph of Sly standing next to the movie poster, and knew I had my money shot that we would publish in the newspaper.

I wanted to ask a question at the press conference, but for some reason I didn't—cold feet, I guess. Instead, Pete asked him about Adrian's absence from the upcoming film. When Sly answered, he turned and spoke directly to us. He said that writing Adrian out of the film was the right thing to do because it was important to show how a great loss affects everyone, even Rocky Balboa. The movie makes a point that we all have to move forward. Stallone had delivered yet another life lesson, but this time it was in person.

When he answered Pete's question it solidified a unique bond between us, the man, and the film. The *Rocky* phenomenon is worldwide, but at this moment, it was hitting home. We were having a *Rocky* conversation with the man who created him. I thought I was the only one who felt the connection, but Pete and Joe did, too. The night kept getting better by the minute.

After the actual press conference, we headed back into the restaurant for cocktails. The center of attention was an incredible ice sculpture of the famous Rocky Statue. Everyone gathered around this shimmering, ice-cold work of art and took turns snapping photographs. Outside, a booth was set up to promote a new product called Sly Glacier Water that was endorsed by Stallone and featured at the event.

As the night progressed, we met a lot of people and made plenty of good contacts. We ran into Frank again and talked about his music career. One of Pete's many hobbies is that he's a drummer, and he connects well with musicians. Joe made sure they each took a photograph of themselves with Frank.

As we moved around the room, I finally met Michael Vitez and Tom Gralish of the *Philadelphia Inquirer* in person. We discussed their book, *Rocky Stories*, and I thanked them again for sending me the information that allowed us to attend this event. Meeting Michael and Tom in person was a good move because they were both in the know and had excellent contacts around Philadelphia. I asked them about the upcoming December premiere and they mentioned that the after-party might be held in this very same Water Works Restaurant and Lounge. I kept that tidbit in mind, and shortly afterward, I met the owner and his wife.

We were having a pleasant conversation next to the Rocky ice sculpture when Sly walked over to talk to the restaurant owner and take a picture with him. His wife didn't have a camera, but she noticed that I did and asked if I would take some photographs. She gave me her e-mail address and begged me to promise I'd send the pictures to her. She thanked me and asked if there was anything she could do for me. I flashed what I'm sure was an enormous grin and jumped all over the opportunity to inquire about the premiere after-party. She said they were making a bid to host the event at their restaurant, and if I e-mailed her the pictures, she would make sure I received an invitation. I said that I would hold her to it and warned that I'm a very persistent person. She laughed and said, "Don't forget to send the photographs."

Once again, I was in the right place at the right time. If the premiere after-party was going to be hosted by my new friends at Water Works Restaurant and Lounge, I knew for sure that I would be a part of it. I was power networking like never before.

Throughout the evening, we ran into Frank several times and had more opportunities to interact with Sly. I took photographs of him with both Pete and Joe. My friends and fellow *Rocky* fans treasured the memory. As the evening began to wind down, Stallone and his entourage left the party. It was time for us to move on to our next adventure, a late-night dinner celebration at Victor Café.

We heard that the now-famous restaurant featured an opera-singing waitstaff and some tasty Italian food. We were seated at a great table with the very same waiter who had startled me back in August when I took a photograph of the café during our family *Rocky* tour as he playfully jumped in front of my camera. I asked if he remembered the incident and explained who I was. He laughed as he recalled the surprised look on my face when he popped out the front door.

We quickly bonded and he even asked me to e-mail him the photograph. Our new Philly friend made sure that our dining experience was fantastic. We peppered him with questions about the filming of the movie at the restaurant, and he gave us some good insight on the whole production. Dinner was delicious, and we pretty much closed the place down as we were the last ones to leave. After our meal, we set out for the two-hour ride back home. We arrived around four that morning, tired, but still glowing with memories of our great adventure.

We came back with some terrific footage of the event and an album full of photographs. When I had them professionally printed, the guy at the shop asked me who I was and how did I get access to these pictures? He was clearly awestruck; apparently they really do look at your photos when they develop them.

I wasted no time e-mailing the pictures of the restaurant owner to his wife and followed up with a telephone call to make sure she had received them. If that premiere after-party was going to be held at their place, then I would definitely be a guest because she appreciated my effort. Everything continued to work in my favor, and I was rolling along with its energy. The uplifting experience of the statue rededication was a *Rocky* high. I continued to attract great opportunities into my life and put myself in the right place at the right time. I knew there would be more to come during the later rounds of my journey.

ROUND TEN

The Plan

With the possibility of the after-party taking place at Water Works Restaurant and Lounge, I continued to formulate my plan. I kept trying to come up with an idea for the promotional marketing proposal. Danny was going to present it to the advertising agency handling the *Rocky* movie, and this idea was my ticket to the premiere.

Unfortunately, I didn't realize that my momentum was about to be interrupted by a large bump in the road. One day in mid-September, Danny came into the office and announced that he had accepted a position at a major sports radio station and was leaving the *Long Island Press*. For weeks he had been hinting that he was going to make this move, but I never took him seriously. I thought he was just talking and would never act upon it. But he was serious—the very next day would be his last at the newspaper. With so much going on at the time, I had to place the *Rocky* promotional proposal on hold.

Busy as I was, I still had to finish the book review on *Rocky Stories* and I began to also write an editorial piece about my Las Vegas experience. I hoped it would find its way into the pages of the newspaper as a cover story. I was creatively occupied, and my attention was divided between work and Rocky. I juggled a lot of everything, but as a man of my word, I tackled the book review first.

As I paged through the *Rocky Stories* book, I came across that guy dressed in the Rocky sweatsuit again. Looking closely at his picture, I remembered that it would make a great Halloween costume. I stored that thought in my memory bank and continued working on the review. The words somehow flowed out of me as if I knew what I was talking about. It was published in our newspaper, and I'm sure it made my Philadelphia friends very happy.

Once an idea comes to me, I usually try to see it through. So a few days later, I stopped off at a local Modell's Sporting Goods store and purchased a traditional grey sweatsuit, a wool cap and black Converse Chuck Taylor sneakers. I continue to believe that things happen for a reason because when I went home to try on my Superman-like outfit, it hit me. The perfect promotional idea came in an instant.

That night I sat down at my computer and banged out one of the greatest proposals I had ever written in all the years of my advertising career. Once again, the words just flowed from my mind to my fingers, skillfully moving over the keyboard. I would take a busload of Long Islanders and dress them up like Rocky in sweatsuit outfits like the one I had just purchased for Halloween. We would all ride to the Philadelphia Museum of Art and run up the famous Rocky Steps simultaneously. Afterward, I would take them to lunch at the famous Pat's King of Steaks, and then we'd do the same mini-tour of *Rocky* sites that my family had visited back in August.

Every step I had taken up to that point seems to have happened for a reason because it all came together in this grand promotional idea. That is exactly what I hoped would eventually get me to the *Rocky Balboa* movie premiere and exclusive after-party.

I then turned to the question of how to finance this exciting excursion. I thought out loud as I typed. Well, I'll get Modell's Sporting Goods to supply all of the sweatsuits, wool hats, sneakers and hand wraps. I'll call one of my oldest clients who owned a limousine company, and ask him to provide free transportation services, just for the fun of taking part in the event. I'll ask Pat's King of Steaks in Philadelphia, people I never met in person, to serve free cheesesteak sandwiches and sodas for lunch. I would use my newfound connection with the Philadelphia Tourism Bureau to help with local media coverage and clearance, if needed. I would even contact the Jakks Pacific Toy Company in California for some *Rocky* toys to use as giveaways, just like they did with a commemorative action figure at the statue dedication. I rationalized that if Jakks did it for the city of Philadelphia, why wouldn't they do the same for me? I even considered contacting Paul Dry Books for complimentary copies of *Rocky Story*. I would also tie in two of our current advertisers, Major World, one of the area's biggest auto dealers, and Miller Brewing Company. Their sponsorship would make it possible for me to run ads to solicit contestants and print a photo wrap-up in the newspaper. I knew that the promise of advertising revenue would easily guarantee the blessing of our publisher.

This whole scenario, which manifested in my head, fell into place to produce a perfectly written proposal. Can you imagine that all of these people and companies, some that I had never met or interacted with, would give me exactly what I asked the universe for? I was so sure the answer would be yes, that as I typed the proposal sentences poured out of me like I had been writing them my whole life. Every word had already been approved by the Law of Attraction, positive thoughts, and my escalating energy.

The promotion was officially dubbed "Yo, Long Island, We Did It!" Now it was time to make it a reality. It helped that I was an experienced media salesman and had been putting promotions together for years. Nothing could stop me now. I selected the Friday after Thanksgiving for the event. The timing was significant because the original *Rocky* was released around Thanksgiving in 1976, and thirty years later we would honor Rocky and Adrian's first date. Every detail was carefully thought out. The printed proposal, complete with cover graphics, was ready to send. I was certain this crazy adventure would lead me to my coveted goal of attending the gala premiere in Philadelphia.

In the whirl of creativity, I momentarily forgot that Danny had already moved on, and I would have to present the proposal to the movie people at the agency myself. This would be my biggest hurdle because I didn't have a relationship with anyone there. I got cold feet and began to second-guess myself.

It occurred to me that Danny might be right; maybe I was out of my mind and going overboard with this whole *Rocky* quest. After all, I was an executive at a successful newspaper company. I had already accomplished the extra thing. Should I really be running around Philadelphia dressed up as Rocky in a grey sweatsuit? Could I pull off a grand promotion that would attract the attention of the movie company and send me to the premiere? My flash of uncertainty came and went as I reassured myself, of course I can. I forged ahead with my plan, energized by those positive thoughts. It was time to take action, the most important component to the Law of Attraction.

My first step was to contact a client named Matt, the owner of a local limousine company, to ask if he would give me a bus to take all these people to Philadelphia. As a trade-off for his services, I would offer to heavily promote his company in the newspaper. Matt understood the power of marketing and quickly agreed. It was a limousine-style bus with wrap-around bench seating that held forty people comfortably, but it would feature a large-screen television.

I had originally considered having seventy-six people in order to commemorate 1976, the year *Rocky* came out. But forty seemed like a more sensible number to work with, and besides, I didn't have a choice. With the limousine bus agreement in place and the number of passengers decided, I continued to pursue this promotion like it was my mission in life. The bonus of having a large-screen television onboard added another dimension. I could now feature the movies *Rocky* and *Rocky II* on the bus rides back and forth, and Pete could lead trivia for prizes. The ideas kept flowing like a faucet that wouldn't turn off.

The next step was to contact Modell's Sporting Goods to ask them to supply forty pairs of grey Russell Athletics sweatsuits, wool hats, and Converse sneakers. But first, I reached out to my contact at Major World to get him involved as a sponsor. Then I asked if he knew anyone at Modell's that I could talk to. The president of Major World was a successful businessman who seemed to know everyone. He gave me the name of the company president at Modell's and said I could use his name as a reference. I immediately called and left a brief message describing the promotion and said I would appreciate one minute of his time to share an idea with him.

What were the chances that I would get a call back? How about one hundred percent! The next day their director of marketing contacted me. He was excited to learn more about my idea. I explained everything, including what I would need from Modell's to make the promotion happen. He asked if I had anything in writing, and I had to smile; I was prepared like never before.

"Of course I do. I'll send it right over."

He said that he was eager to see the proposal so he could run it past a few people in his organization. Minutes later, it was on its way. We discussed the details over the next few days, and then he called back with Modell's terms and conditions. I braced myself as he spelled out their additional demands. The hooded sweatshirts would have to show the Russell Athletics logo on the front, and Modell's logo on the back.

"Done deal," I said.

The wool hats had to have Modell's logo on the front.

"Done deal."

They wanted all of the sneaker sizes as far in advance as possible.

"Done deal," I said, even though it would be a huge hassle. I would have to work out those details later on.

Lastly, he said that he had contacted Everlast for the hand wraps, and they would get involved only if they could also give us forty pairs of real-leather Rocky boxing gloves that were about to hit the market, along with a box of posters.

"Are you kidding me?" I practically shouted, "Done deal!"

So that was it. Modell's was an official sponsor. Not only were they a part of the promotion, but they were coming to the table with a lot of terrific extras. My Law of Attraction magnet was pulling in the right direction again. I received everything I needed from them, plus extra giveaways.

I was rolling now. My next step was to contact the owner of Pat's King of Steaks, the famous Philly cheesesteak stand that had appeared in the original *Rocky*. I wish this went easy, too, but I had to work hard for this one. I made a few calls and left messages, but no one ever called back. Eventually, I managed to get the owner's name, Frank Olivieri Jr., from someone who finally answered my call, so I felt like I was on the right track.

As I waited for a callback from Mr. Olivieri, I moved forward with the next step by contacting Jakks Pacific, a toy company in California. I had called them earlier in the year about highlighting the *Rocky* action figures they were going to launch around the release of the film in our holiday gift guide feature in the newspaper. I didn't know then why I made that call, but now I realized it was to land forty pairs of Rocky boxing gloves that make lifelike action sounds. It was accomplished with a single call to this large, national toy company.

By now, I was more motivated than ever. The next call was to a longtime client, the local beer distributor. I described what we were trying to pull off, and my request for Miller Beer's involvement produced an immediate yes. They agreed to sponsor the photo wrap-up that would take place at the Philadelphia Museum of Art. It would be featured as a center spread in our newspaper. I also learned from our editor that we would dedicate an issue to *Rocky*. It would include my Las Vegas editorial, "On the Set of *Rocky Balboa,*" as a cover story, along with our promotional wrap-up. The editor had told our publisher that my story was "surprisingly charming."

Piece by piece, I somehow produced one Rocky feat after another. I now concentrated on enhancing the promotion. I contacted Paul Dry Books to request a box of complimentary copies of *Rocky Story* to utilize as prizes for our *Rocky* quiz during the bus ride, and of course, I received another positive response.

I then returned my focus to Pat's King of Steaks and placed two more calls, with no luck in reaching the owner. Was my good fortune running out? I remained persistent and optimistic. On the third try, someone actually answered the phone and said if I wanted to speak to him I needed to call back at 2 p.m. I did as instructed and reached Frank, Jr. himself. I quickly explained what I was trying to accomplish and asked for forty free sandwiches and sodas. I thought he would surely think I was crazy, but had confidence that he would respond positively to my request.

"Are you from Long Island?" he asked.

"Yes."

"I have a friend from Long Island," he said. "He's a very good divorce lawyer."

In a strange twist of fate related to the Law of Attraction, one of my clients was currently reigning as the "Best of LI Divorce Lawyer" for that year. Without hesitation, I asked "Is it Anthony Capetola?"

There was a pause and then he said, "Yes, how do you know Tony?"

My eyes and mouth popped wide open; I couldn't believe my ears. Of all the lawyers on Long Island, we both knew the same person, the exact one that I spontaneously mentioned. When I explained how I knew him, the owner of Pat's King of Steaks said to me, "Any friend of Tony's is a friend of mine. No problem, the lunch is on me."

He asked me to e-mail the details and call him two days before the promotion as a reminder. He ended the conversation by saying that he looked forward to meeting me. I hung up the phone in total amazement. I had just called the owner of one the most famous eateries in the United States, and I received exactly what I asked for because we both knew the very same person. What a crazy circle of influence the universe provides.

Everything continued to fall into place. All I needed now was to pitch my idea to someone at the advertising agency for the movie company. I was confident this person would be floored to have such an incredible promotion dropped into their lap, and as my reward, he would say, "Now I'm going to take you to the premiere in Philadelphia."

I thought it would be easy, but this request didn't turn out the way I expected. Sometimes things don't go your way for a reason. I think when that happens, it's because the Law of Attraction has something better in store for you.

I called the advertising agency and spoke to the man who handled the Sony Pictures account. He was initially interested and asked me to send a copy of the proposal. He would have to run it by Sony for their approval, and that could take weeks. It was already nearing the middle of November, and the promotion launch was just days away. We didn't have weeks to spare, so I pushed him to get an answer as soon as possible. I sent him a sample of the advertisement to announce the promotion, and an hour later he called back. They wanted me to change quite a few details and offered different reasons for each one. Every time I made a correction to the ad, I sent back an edited draft for his approval. I was driving our production department crazy, but was fortunate to be working with a very understanding designer. He knew how important this was to me and did me a favor by changing the advertisement often and getting it done quickly for each phase of the approval process. When it was finalized, everything seemed to be in place and ready to go. The advertisement invited *Long Island Press* readers to be a part of this inspiring experience.

I was now at deadline and still waiting for the go-ahead from the agency. We had to run the ad the very next day to give it two full weeks of promotion, both to help me do right by the sponsors, and to allow enough time for me to line up all of the participants. I waited anxiously to hear back from the agency. Then I placed another call. When I finally got him on the telephone, he didn't give me the answer I was looking for. He insisted that the advertisement could not run without permission from the movie company. So what was supposed to be the easiest part of this adventure was quickly turning into a nightmare.

My deadline passed that evening, without receiving the approval. The promotion and advertisement from that week's issue of the newspaper had to be pulled. The agency guy didn't seem to get it, and he sure didn't care about the sense of urgency. I was furious at him because we had changed the advertisement four times at his request to make it as generic as possible. I was annoyed and disappointed, but I still had to appear professional. Looking forward, I was counting on this guy for my ticket to the premiere; I didn't want to risk damaging our relationship by spewing out my frustration.

Finally the decision to cancel the promotion was made, and all of the hard work seemed like a huge waste of effort. Without two solid weeks of marketing, there was no way it could happen. I dreaded having to inform everyone involved. My first step was to tell Jed, the publisher of the paper, that I was pulling the plug.

"Why do that?" he asked. "You worked hard on this promotion, and everything is set. Just move the date back two weeks so you can get the approval."

Jed talked some sense into me, even though my mind was stuck on that Thanksgiving date. When I come up with an idea, it stays in my head, and it's tough for me to change my course of action. I wanted the event to happen on that November weekend, but I knew he was right: There was only one choice. The date was pushed back two weeks to December 9th. With that decision made, the sponsors were called to advise them of the new details, and to get their approval. I was nervous about the availability of the bus but the limousine company made it happen for us.

I then turned my attention back to the agency guy. But as the next deadline approached, I was faced with the exact same situation—still didn't have their approval. I had made all those phone calls changing the date, and no way was I going to hold back again. Another frustrating deadline passed as I waited for the go ahead. When it didn't happen, I debated calling a halt on the entire promotion, this time for good.

Jed and I had another déjà vu conversation, and we agreed to proceed without an official blessing from the agency or the movie company. I was determined to press on, and nothing was going to hold me back. I would stick to my plan and go for it on December 9th. I knew I was taking a big chance and probably burning a bridge with the agency. The decision to go forward had to be made because my determination could no longer be contained.

I placed the advertisement in the newspaper, and the *Rocky* promotion was officially on. The ad came out the next day, and by 11 a.m. we had our first e-mail entry. They poured in all day long, and we received way more than needed during the next week. I easily had forty qualified people within a day or two. My assistant and I called every applicant to confirm their availability as a passenger since they would need to guarantee their attendance.

Each person shared a great story as to why they wanted to be part of this adventure. Some had overcome an illness, some had achieved successful weight loss, and others had suffered a breakup, or just wanted to feel the combined energy, but the bottom line was that they were all *Rocky* fans. They had one goal, and their intention was to hit that top step and thrust their arms up in victory. Everyone understood the significance of this trip to the famous steps and responded to the same purpose. It was simply amazing. In the end, we found some of the most compatible, friendly people and we were happy to have them join us.

Our decision to go ahead without the agency probably ruined any chance to ask for help in regards to the premiere. But I did what I had to do. Too much time had already been spent, and too many people were involved; we simply could no longer wait for the official approval. I didn't want to limit my chances, but knew that I was destined to attend the premiere and would get there somehow.

By this time, I also learned that the Water Works Restaurant and Lounge would not be hosting the after-party. Instead, it would be held inside the Philadelphia Museum of Art, just beyond those same Rocky Steps. That was another letdown, but I still had faith. When you want something, you have to hold positive thoughts about it, because sometimes the answer is only a few doors away.

The past summer at our annual, neighborhood block party, I'd had a discussion about *Rocky* with my neighbor Frank who lives two doors away. He's is a great guy and works in the movie industry as a studio executive. Not only are we current neighbors, but we had also lived five blocks from each other when we were kids. We never met back in the old days, but something brought us together and I'm sure glad it did.

I updated him on my *Rocky* adventures every time I saw him. At the block party, he mentioned that he might be able to help me get to the premiere, and I should remind him as the date got closer. When the promotion came out in the paper, I remembered that conversation. I told him what happened with the agency guy, and he offered to call some of his contacts to see if they could hook me up.

Everything seemed to be back on track, and the two-week delay worked in my favor. We were faced with a few challenges to overcome, including a last-minute insurance concern and other twists and hurdles. First, the participants were to meet at 5 a.m. at a local diner where we had arranged for a free breakfast and parking. But the diner reneged after the first week of the promotion, so I had to act fast to change the breakfast plan and our starting location. We would now gather at our office at the same time on the morning of the ninth. Participants would be given their instructions for the day, sign their insurance waiver, and receive a large goodie bag filled with giveaways and accessories. I treated everyone to coffee and doughnuts instead of the diner breakfast. This change in plans was advantageous, since everyone now had a safe place to park their car. I managed to work out a deal with a local restaurant called 13A to give us a smoked rib dinner when we returned as a way to wrap up the day's events. I figured the ribs tied in well with the famous beef punching scene. All the participants were happy because it added another benefit to the promotion—and they didn't stop there.

Days before the event, in another Law-of-Attraction moment, our editor gave me the name of a public relations firm handling the launch of a repackaged, commemorative DVD of the original *Rocky*. This special edition product was set to go on sale during the holiday season, just in time for the release of *Rocky Balboa*. The editor said they were looking for some coverage on the DVD in our newspaper. Plus, they could arrange for us to conduct telephone interviews with actors Burt Young and Dolph Lundgren to help promote it. The editor had heard my *Rocky* story so many times that he had no doubt I was the man to assist one of our reporters with the interviews. He was right about that, and I could not have been more excited. This gave me another chance to interact with Mr. Young.

I called the public relations company to confirm our plans for the interviews. While I was talking to the gentleman, I happened to mention my upcoming Philly promotion. The more I talked about it, the more intrigued he became. Without my even asking, he offered to give me forty copies of the commemorative DVD for the giveaway bags. Do you believe this? Everything continued to come my way. Not only did we have additional giveaways, but we now had a special DVD to show on the big screen aboard the bus. The Law-of-Attraction magic had struck again.

After working out the DVD details, I was given instructions for the interview. The man said that Burt was working on a project in Rome so he would set up a three-way call for us to reach him. As for Dolph, he gave me his home telephone number in London so we could contact him at our leisure. I was blown away. The same Law of Attraction had just delivered Ivan Drago's home telephone number in the palm of my hand. He also suggested that we reach out to Jimmy Gambina, who was Stallone's original boxing trainer and played the role of Mike the cornerman.

Over the next two days, I helped one of our staff reporters named Tom with the interviews. When we spoke to Burt, I got the feeling that he remembered me after I once again reminded him of that old diner story. We had a great conversation, even though I already knew some of his answers from speaking to him in Vegas and articles I'd read about him or heard from my godfather. He comes across as a good-hearted person who speaks his mind. He told us some things I wasn't aware of, such as his feelings toward Talia Shire, and how much the turkey scene in the original film had affected him. He claimed it was a difficult scene for him emotionally because it was so intense. Burt worried that he was hurting her every time he threw the turkey out the door during the many takes. The interview was informative, and at the end we even asked him for advice on running the Rocky Steps when we did our promotion. "Yes, run them carefully," he said.

The next day, we called Dolph in London. We couldn't get over the fact that we were talking to Ivan Drago on the telephone at his home. We were star struck throughout the entire interview. It was cool finding out how he got the part to star in *Rocky IV*. Lundgren was initially rejected by Stallone's ex-wife Sasha for being too tall, but he managed to get a second look by Sly himself. He said Stallone loved his act of saying practically nothing as he just stood there looking menacing and intimidating. Dolph believed that helped land the role because it made him stand out among the other boisterous hopefuls.

Our reporter handled the Gambina interview by himself and gained some great insight about making the films, especially the boxing training. Gambina was on the front lines because he was both a boxing trainer and an actor. He gave us a real insider's look into the original *Rocky*.

After the interviews, we turned our full attention to the promotion. My assistant and I went through the contestant list and peppered each person to make sure they "double guaranteed" to show up. We made arrangements through the Philadelphia Tourism Bureau for media coverage and touted the fact that we would have forty Rocky dress-alikes from Long Island arriving at those steps.

As the date drew closer, I contacted Michael Vitez to request coverage from the *Philadelphia Enquirer*. After discussing the finalized details, Mike kindly invited me to his book-release event at—yes—the top of the Rocky Steps. He mentioned that a cast member from *Rocky Balboa* might show up as a guest. I immediately called Pete, and without hesitation, we hit the road on our third trip of the year to the Rocky Steps. It was getting to be routine for us, and we certainly didn't need directions any more.

The book signing turned out to be a nice affair featuring some of the people Vitez acknowledged in his book, along with Geraldine Hughes, a newcomer to the cast. She played little Marie, a main character in *Rocky Balboa*. I had met her previously in Las Vegas, but she didn't remember me. We chatted for awhile, and I told her about our plans to run a group of people from Long Island up the same steps that we were standing on within the next week. Geraldine lived in Manhattan and said she was intrigued by the promotion. I invited her to join us on the bus, and she expressed an interest. But when she told me to e-mail her publicist with the information, I knew she was just trying to be polite, and I didn't expect anything to come of it. I followed through with the publicist, and I was right, we never heard back from her.

Visiting the steps for a third time that year provided a great chance to network, and Vitez was an excellent contact. When we left that day, I casually mentioned that I would see him at the premiere, and he asked if I had tickets.

"Not yet."

Michael smiled politely, and I wondered if he thought I stood the slightest chance of attending. He didn't know me well enough to understand my persistence, but he knew I was motivated when it came to Rocky.

Our elaborate *Long Island Press* promotion was now just days away, and we had issued several press releases. Although we lost our morning meeting spot, we had gained a dinner and two new sponsors. Besides the new restaurant, we also secured a fitness studio to help us with a morning workout in Modell's parking lot to prepare us for our big run up the steps. My coworker Harlan hooked me up with an independent movie producer named Jarett who agreed to shoot a professional, fifteen-minute video of our adventure for practically nothing. People were stepping up from every direction, and all things *Rocky* kept coming like magic, with only a few minor bumps in the road.

We contacted the participants one final time to confirm the starting point at our office and the new plan for breakfast. Most of the giveaways and equipment arrived during that last week, including the large shipment of outfits from Modell's.

On the Friday night before the promotion, my assistant and I worked overtime to prepare for the event. We went to the Modell's in Farmingdale to organize our system for passing out the sweatsuits, hats and sneakers, hoping for a smooth transition when all forty of us arrived to get dressed. It was tricky making sure all the sizes were right. There were so many details to consider, and it was complicated to pull off. I could hardly sleep the night before the big event. But we were all set, and our itinerary was mapped out. Every detail had been timed down to the very second; we were ready for the bell to signal the start of the next round.

On the big day, I woke up at 4 a.m. and slipped on my official Modell's-sponsored Rocky outfit, which included the grey Russell sweatpants and hooded pullover. I tied up my black Converse Chuck Taylors, put on my wool cap, and placed a light blue towel around my neck. Chrissy cut forty towels to perfection from a roll of cloth she found at the local fabric store, just to honor my insane desire for detail. I was ready. The executive in me was long gone, and I was officially transformed into a Rocky disciple.

I left my house in the early dawn, just like Rocky did in his original workout scene. It was a crisp and refreshing December morning. As I saw my frozen breath in the air, it gave me a strange but familiar feeling that reminded me of that time in Las Vegas when my sister drove me to the bus at the gentlemen's club.

Next, I headed to the office and stopped at Dunkin' Donuts to pick up some treats and coffee for breakfast. Then it was over to the office to set up everything by 5:30 a.m. A team of helpers, including some of the *Press* staff, Pete, Joe, and another childhood friend Rob, were waiting for me. I always included my friends in these *Rocky* adventures, so naturally they had to be a part of this crazy experience.

I was pleased that my coworkers jumped onboard because it showed they had an interest in my little fantasy world. They all helped out in a big way, especially with the setup that morning so we could start on time.

My assistant was assigned to check people in and have them sign permission slips. He was unaware that his voice tended to be a little loud, especially when his adrenaline got going. I was upstairs in my office getting the giveaway bags together, and he was downstairs yelling at everyone for their consent sheets during the roll call. One of my other coworkers came running up the stairs to tell me I'd better hurry down before the sleepy crowd of contestants decked him in the first boxing match of the day.

I hustled down to calm everyone and handle the first bump in the road. We then got the rest of the goodie bags ready, and the group was floored when they saw the number and quality of their gifts. I gave everyone the option of putting their bag in their car or taking it along for the ride so they could use things like the boxing gloves as props for the pictures when we ran the Rocky Steps.

It was a pleasure meeting all the contestants in person. I had already spoken to most of them by phone and learned about the interesting reasons they wanted to go on the trip, so it was like seeing old friends again. We were all on the same wavelength, and on this day, we shared boundless energy.

After roll call, we found out that one person had not shown up, so we had an extra seat available. Fortunately, the husband of one of the participants, a nice woman named Kim wanted to be included in the worst way. Her husband Bob stuck around, hoping for an empty seat, and he got one. He probably manifested his opportunity without realizing it. They were the nicest couple and had such a heartwarming story. Kim had bounced back from a serious illness, and reaching the top of the Rocky Steps would signify that she had made it all the way back to good health. Having her husband along made her personal journey even more special. Almost everyone on the bus had a heartwarming story, which gave special meaning to hitting the top of those steps. I felt like I was meant to deliver this program to these lucky winners.

The bus arrived fifteen minutes early at 6:15 a.m., beautifully lit with neon lights that glowed in the early-morning dawn. I briefed everyone about what to expect from the day's festivities. We were ahead of schedule and things were looking good as Jarett, the video guy, rolled tape and all of us boarded the bus.

When everyone looked for a place to sit on the leather, wraparound bench, we noticed our next situation of the day. There was only room for thirty-seven people. As I assessed the problem, it was quickly solved by my coworker named Jon, who volunteered himself and two others to follow behind in their own car. I was sorry they wouldn't be on the bus with us, but they insisted it was the best plan. Little did I realize that later in the day it would prove to be the perfect plan.

With the seating arrangements taken care of, we were fully packed and ready to begin our journey. It was just after 7 a.m. when we pulled away from our parking lot, giving us enough time to drive the twenty minutes to the nearby Modell's location. Once there, our task was to suit up everyone with their Rocky outfits and sneakers, sharing the few available dressing rooms. Outfitting forty people under these conditions was not an easy undertaking. It would probably be the most difficult part of the day—at least that's what I assumed.

We had arranged everything in order of size the night before, but all that went by the wayside as sweatsuits and sneakers went flying this way and that. It seemed that everyone had either a pair of pants or a shirt that was too big or too small, and the different-sized sneakers were tough to figure out. The Modell's manager was really helpful, especially in exchanging some of the sneaker sizes we were having trouble with. It didn't seem to matter how much planning and preparation we had done, everyone was trading something for a different size while getting dressed. What a wild scene this chaos would have made for a movie—and with Jarett still filming, I guess it did.

Finally, everyone was ready to go, and the excitement level zoomed. We were all charged up with energy by the simple act of putting on grey sweatsuits and those sneakers. We headed outside to be put through a warm-up program led by the fitness studio guy. We did push-ups and ran around the parking lot together. It was a sight to see as most of us dress-alikes struggled with the exercises, including me, but we were still pumped. I had arranged for television news coverage at Modell's, but when it didn't happen, I just resigned myself. Oh well, I thought, no time to be let down now, and besides, Jarett captured all of the action.

We boarded the bus again, as upbeat as ever, and within minutes we were officially off to Philadelphia. As we drove away, the original *Rocky* movie started scrolling across the big screen in the back of the bus. I can't begin to describe how fantastic we felt about our big day. The theme music was blaring, and we couldn't wait to run those steps.

The plan was for us to drive straight through. I had made the trip so many times recently that I knew exactly how long it would take to get there. I figured we would arrive by 12 noon. I had corresponded numerous times with the Philadelphia Travel & Tourism Bureau to request media coverage, and they assured me someone would meet us when we arrived.

The bus ride was going well. Some passengers slept, some continued to watch the movie, some chatted with new friends, and others answered trivia questions for giveaway prizes. We were having a blast.

As we drove through the New Jersey countryside, my cell phone rang. It was my co-worker Jon, who was in a car traveling behind us. "Felice, I think you have a problem with one of the bus tires. Maybe you should stop and check it out; it doesn't look right."

Now I am the most stubborn guy, especially when I have a plan in my head. I was determined that we would arrive at the steps by 12 noon so we could meet the media, do our run, take photographs, be at Pat's King of Steaks for a 2 p.m. lunch, and do our *Rocky* tour afterwards.

"I don't feel anything," I told him. "It seems like we're all right, and we're so close to being on schedule. We'll try to make it and check out the tires when we get there."

Jon warned me against that plan, urging us to stop and check the tires. When I still resisted, he said it was my call, so we continued on. About five minutes later, he called again.

"Felice, that tire is a mess. We really need to pull into the next rest area and take a look at those tires. Something's not right."

We pulled over at a rest stop just down the road, and everyone exited the bus while the driver and I surveyed the situation. Sure enough, Jon was right. The bus had double tires on each side of the axle, and one of the inside back tires on the passenger side was shredding apart. As we debated what to do, the Rocky dress-alikes took the opportunity to run into the rest stop together. I could only imagine the look of surprise on the faces of fellow travelers when all those *Rocky* fans invaded the building.

My attention quickly returned to the tire predicament and how to best handle the situation. I talked it over with the bus driver, my three friends, and coworkers. We were about thirty minutes away from Philadelphia, and since the inside back tire was giving us the problem, but the outside tire was fine, the bus driver suggested we continue on. He believed we could make it on the one tire. The driver said that he would call ahead to the mechanic and have him meet us at the steps. He could fix the tire while we were doing our thing.

You didn't have to tell me, "Mr. Stubborn," twice. Of course I thought it was a great idea. After all, it was coming from the bus driver, so I took his advice. Everybody climbed back on the bus, and we headed toward our ultimate destination. As we pulled out of the parking lot, I kept telling myself that we simply had to arrive on schedule, but I was also concerned for the safety of our passengers. The driver seemed confident we could make it, and he had all the experience, so I felt comfortable with the decision to proceed. No more than seven minutes down the road, my cell phone rang again, and it was Jon.

"Felice, we really have a big problem. Rubber is flying all over the road. You better pull over."

"But, Jon," I protested. "We're so close. Let's just stick to the bus driver's plan."

"You should pull over," he repeated.

About thirty seconds later, we stopped for a red light at an intersection in Cherry Hill, New Jersey. I was startled by someone banging on the front door of the bus. It was Jon. The door opened, and I saw the look of near-panic on his face.

"Felice, you have got to pull over. There's more rubber flying everywhere, and now some kind of fluid is draining all over the road and hitting the windshield of our car."

That's all he had to say. The very fact that he got out of his car finally convinced me that we could no longer continue. We pulled over immediately at the intersection, and everyone got out again. We saw a major pool of power steering fluid draining from the bus. We officially had a problem—a really big one—and I had to figure out what we should do next because everyone's safety was a concern. Running those steps now took a backseat to the situation at hand.

We surveyed the extensive damage and knew we were screwed. It was almost noon, and here we were, stranded on this grass island in Cherry Hill, New Jersey on the outskirts of Philadelphia. As forty people dressed like Rocky Balboa stood by the side of the road, I wasn't sure where the rest of the day was going. As I thought out loud to my friends, the bus driver called for roadside assistance. It would take awhile for the mobile truck repairman to show up, and we had to wait our turn.

The passengers looked to me for a plan on this now-frigid December afternoon. The bus driver said that since the draining liquid was only power steering fluid, we could wait in the bus. I instructed everyone to get out of the cold and warm up inside until helped arrived. I was trying to make responsible decisions, especially with the insurance liability thing on my mind. So we all boarded and sat in the bus, patiently awaiting our next move. My friends entertained us with some of their antics; they all have a great sense of humor and very good timing. Someone had asked them where we were. Joe pointed to the right on the map and replied, "I think we're here." Rob then pointed left and said, "Yeah, but our tire is over there." It seemed like everyone was a part of the adventure for a reason and my friends provided some entertainment when we needed it the most. The guys are pretty funny, and I was sure glad they had joined us that day.

When help finally arrived about thirty minutes later, we had to stand outside in the cold again until the problem was fixed. We discovered that the flat tire had shredded and ripped out the power steering line; it was a mess. Waiting outside, our guests were cold and hungry. It was already past noon and heading toward 1 p.m. A jumble of thoughts swirled around in my mind. First of all, we had blown the media coverage at the steps. I tried to think of alternate ways to get us there, including walking, but that was a dumb idea. I considered riding in taxi cabs, but I didn't want to split everyone up. We were facing some adversity, but to my surprise, most of the group shared a determination and desire to go the distance.

It turned out to be a stroke of good luck after all that my coworkers had followed us in a separate car. They got to witness the whole tire-shredding incident right in front of them. Being stranded, we were also fortunate to have someone with a car to drive ahead and bring us back some hot coffee and pizza to keep us warm and filled up. They took real good care of us.

The repair man eventually showed up and went to work on the bus. He made a quick assessment of the task at hand and said we would be there for quite awhile. I'm sure a look of disappointment flashed across my face. I was now pacing in earnest. My itinerary was completely messed up, plus I was responsible for everyone's safety. The clock kept ticking, and we were supposed to be heading to Pat's King of Steaks for our cheesesteak lunch at this time. Instead, we were stuck on the side of the road in New Jersey, eating pizza and sipping hot coffee from cardboard cups. Everyone was coming up to me individually to ask my thoughts, and Jarett was still catching the whole fiasco on film. Ironically, he was shooting a short feature to mix with some *Rocky* footage and music from the actual movies. In a parallel path, we were also facing major adversity, and our own *Rocky* story was going to make one heck of a production.

It took nearly three frustrating hours to finish the repairs. One of the dirtiest mechanics in the world was lying on the ground, rolling around in power steering fluid. He was actually smoking a cigarette while working on the bus. The day was totally in turmoil, so I gathered my friends in for another huddle and a meeting of the minds.

"What should we do," I asked. "Should we continue?"

As we weighed our options, a group of our passengers listening in on the conversation shouted, "Continue! We have to continue and run those steps, no matter what."

It was unanimous. The universal sentiment held that this was an adventure and a challenge—just like *Rocky*. We had gotten knocked down. Now we had to dig in deep, revise our plans, and figure out how to go the distance. The group was now functioning as one unit and sharing a single thought process. We were more determined than ever to reach our goal at the top of those steps. It was an amazing moment, one that united us and pulled us together as a team. It was as if the *Rocky* music had just started playing in my head.

Of course I agreed to continue on, especially after the bus driver reassured us that the mechanic was terrific and was getting the job done. All I had to do was revise the itinerary. I told Pete that nothing could stop us now, and he quipped, "We'll make it as long as that mechanic doesn't kill us smoking his cigarette over the power steering fluid by that gas line."

I don't know why I laughed at that, but I was relieved enough to find some humor in it. As Jarett's video camera rolled, Pete broke into a song parody, "Gonna Die Now," making up lyrics to the tune of the *Rocky* theme song.

After finishing pizza and coffee, the dress-a-likes started getting restless;

they were anxious for the mechanic to finish so we could be on our way. To my surprise, some of them took out the giveaway boxing gloves and sparred with each other. It was a comical sight. Passing motorists honked their horns or yelled out comments to this group of apparent Rocky boxers who were mixing it up alongside the busy street.

We continued to pass the time, and everybody remained stalwart in their conviction that we needed to carry on, again comparing our situation to the way Rocky overcame his battles. We stayed focused on the goal of running those steps. We just had to get there. It was 3 p.m. by the time we finally hit the road again, headed for the Philadelphia Museum of Art. I was so relieved that the bus was finally moving and we were on our way at last. I looked into the camera, "Thank goodness we're rolling."

I took roll call and announced our new itinerary. By then we were battling daylight; it would be dark just before 5 p.m. Our group would head directly to the Rocky Steps and stay there for only a half hour. We had to act quickly once we arrived. There would be limited time for individual photographs if we wanted to take a group shot at the top of the steps and another one by the Rocky statue that Miller Beer was sponsoring. These photos were supposed to be published in the *Long Island Press*.

Since daylight was running out and we had already eaten pizza for lunch, I called Pat's King of Steaks and told them to expect us for dinner instead. That switch bought us some time to visit other popular sites such as the pet store, Mighty Mick's Gym, and Rocky's apartment while it was still relatively light out. After our cheesesteak dinner, we could take a quick run down the streets of the famous Philadelphia Italian Market. Rocky had run down South 9th Street where a street vendor flipped him an orange during the training montage in the original film. After the Italian Market, we would head back home for a late-night victory celebration at the restaurant where some free barbecued beef ribs would be waiting for us.

As we approached the Philadelphia Museum of Art, our spirits were soaring once again. It was astonishing how the breakdown of the bus and the adversity we faced back in Cherry Hill only added to the buildup of this climactic moment. We could all feel how special it was. There is definitely something energizing about those steps that you feel as soon as you see the statue of George Washington on his horse. Just beyond it is the bronze statue of Rocky next to those seventy-two glorious steps.

When the bus stopped, everyone started chanting, "Rocky, Rocky, Rocky." It was crazy. Even my coworkers, who I thought were just amused by my enthusiasm, were over-the-top excited to run those steps. It was fun for me to see their reaction. I believe there really is a little Rocky in all of us.

I reminded everyone about the photo plan and the meager amount of daylight left for our other scheduled activities. Of course by this time, no media coverage was waiting for us. In fact, I'm not even sure whether or not they showed up in the first place. But we had made it, so no one really cared; the moment was all ours. Running those steps was the only thing that mattered now.

All of us dressed like Rocky Balboa presented quite a memorable scene. Other tourists wanted to take pictures of us, but there was something we had to do first. We were on a mission. As we approached the bottom of the steps, this special moment meant something different to each of us. To me it represented success in pulling off this incredible project with all the hard work, planning and effort. It was now obvious that my brilliant promotion would not lead me to obtain a ticket to the premiere or the after-party, but it didn't matter anymore—it was all positive, and we were feeling the energy of this experience. This was what the movie stood for, and we were filled with Rocky Spirit.

We looked up toward the top step, took a collective deep breath, and counted to three. With a running start, we charged up those steps together as one unit. I wondered if I would ever have an opportunity to do something like that again. I was even more curious what the others were thinking. I got my answer when we reached the top and everyone—and I do mean everyone—danced around like crazy, raising their arms in victory, just like Rocky Balboa. It was a thrill, and my joy was indescribable. We were all screaming and chanting as Jarett captured the moment on video. We posed for a group photograph on top of the steps that was later published under the title, "Yo, Long Island, We Did It." I'm certain that a copy of that photograph still hangs on a few walls to this day.

After the group photo, we each ran the steps individually for the video and then headed to the Rocky statue for another picture. We also took time to oblige the other tourists who wanted to take photographs with us. Our positive energy was making their day. Back on the bus, our next goal was to finish the tour while we still had some daylight and see the rest of the *Rocky* sites on the itinerary.

Our first stop was at Mighty Mick's Gym and the pet shop storefront across the street. We stared out the windows as we passed familiar backgrounds from some of the movies. Unfortunately, we didn't have time to get off the bus at this point because we wanted to run down the street where Rocky's apartment was located.

It was turning dark when we arrived at the address, 1818 Tusculum Street, in the heart of Philadelphia. We piled off the bus and jogged down the street toward his apartment. It was euphoria all over again. The building looked almost exactly as it did in the original film more than thirty years ago. The excitement of being at this historic location took our adventure to another high. Our commotion aroused the neighborhood, and many of the residents came out to see what was going on. We were polite, and they treated us well, encouraging us to have fun. I had the opportunity to briefly talk to the owner of the building who lived a few doors away. I wondered what it was like to live on that famous block and whether they ever watched any of the movies. Did they welcome the attention their neighborhood received?

It was now dark, and wanting to be respectful of the neighbors, I urged everyone to return to the bus after about fifteen minutes. Our next stop was a dinner date with the best Philly cheesesteak stand in the world, Pat's King of Steaks. It became even more famous after that scene from the original movie where Rocky and Tony Gazzo were standing in front of the restaurant. The actual spot is commemorated with a bronze plaque on the sidewalk in front of the pickup window.

When we arrived at Pat's, we crossed the street together to stand in a line that already stretched around the corner. All eyes were fixed on our forty Rocky dress-alikes. I jumped ahead to make sure we were welcome and the deal was still on for our complimentary meal. The gentleman behind the counter, John the night manager, claimed to know nothing about a free meal. That caused the smile on my face to disappear instantly. I couldn't believe it. I had arranged everything for lunch, but when the plan changed to dinner, no one bothered to tell the night manager. I urged John to please check with the owner, and he obliged. One of his guys made the call, and minutes later, my smile returned—everything was good to go. We were treated to free cheesesteak sandwiches and soft drinks, prepared to perfection.

He asked if we wanted them "wit" onions and Cheez Whiz, the extra toppings that make Pat's legendary sandwich a true American experience. This Philadelphia favorite never tasted so good. I was pleased to watch our group enjoy the treat, and I couldn't have been more grateful to Mr. Olivieri and our friends at Pat's King of Steaks.

After this delicious meal, we headed over to South 9th Street to visit Philadelphia's unique Italian Market district. But it was late, so the vendor carts were empty, shops were closed, and the streets deserted. Most of us were completely exhausted from the day's activities, but we still wanted to run through these famous streets where the Southpaw from Philly had trained. Afterward, we climbed back onto the bus, ready for the return trip home.

When we arrived, more food was waiting for us at a new steak and ribs restaurant called 13A. We were treated to a championship meal consisting of a mountain of barbecued beef ribs. Those of us who could stay broke bread together and enjoyed a final bonding experience with our new friends. In spite of the challenges, it turned out to be an extraordinary promotion that offered a little bit of everything. We were sad to see the day come to an end, but looked forward to getting together in a few weeks to watch the edited video of our *Rocky* adventure.

Completing this journey was a fulfilling moment for me that proved once again the power of positive thinking. I absolutely knew that if I put my mind to something, there was no stopping me—I could accomplish anything. It was this thought process that empowered me to complete the amazing promotion, cover story and wrap-up in the newspaper that would hit the stands a few days later on December 14th.

I learned a lot about the combined efforts of like-minded people and how we could share a higher energy. Everything was becoming more interesting, along with an unknown of where it would take me next. I kept my thoughts on task, and that was to attend the premiere and after party beyond the same Rocky Steps that just energized our group to the highest level. This all prepared me for the next round of the journey.

ROUND ELEVEN

Golden Ticket

Even though the grand promotion had been successful, it didn't accomplish the end result I was looking for: a ticket to the premiere and an invitation to the after-party. But I knew in my heart that I would still find a way somehow, and I devoted my full attention to that goal. My neighbor and his contacts in the movie business were my only hope.

More than the first week of December passed and the premiere was only a week away. Time was running short, so I started putting a lot of pressure on Frank. I must have asked him for an update every time I saw him. One day when I went outside, he saw me and ducked back into his house to avoid speaking to me. That was a none-too-subtle sign telling me to back off, which I did. Still, I knew that he would come through for me. He simply had to come through for me. My conviction was so strong that throughout the day I would envision myself partying with Sly, Burt, and the rest of the gang at the event.

It was now December 14th, just four days shy of the gala. I noticed Frank outside and was reluctant to approach him, but I did anyway. I asked if he had any good news for me, expecting to hear another "Not yet." But he was beaming, and announced, "You're going! And check this out, not only did I get you two tickets for the premiere and the after-party, I actually landed you the president of MGM's seats."

I was shocked and I didn't believe him at first. Frank explained that he had called in a big favor, and I lucked out. The head of MGM couldn't make it to the event, so I was getting his seats and his invitation. It was official! Frank—my neighbor, friend, and new hero—had just given me the most unbelievable news ever. I had been manifesting this in my head for the longest time, and now I had the incredible bonus of getting the top man's prestigious tickets. Another *Rocky* miracle had just happened to me. Frank said that a nice woman with a charming accent would contact me the next day with all the details. I couldn't wait to share this amazing news with Chrissy. I hugged Frank and thanked him.

The next day, my home phone rang, and when I picked it up, I heard this very pleasant voice. It was a nice woman calling me for my contact information so she could e-mail the invitation and details. She confirmed that Frank had facilitated the arrangement, and they were, indeed, the president of MGM's personal seats. She thanked me and said to follow the directions in her e-mail; the actual tickets would be waiting for me at the will call table at the theater under my name.

This phone call was another extraordinary experience in my string of great *Rocky* moments. Everything continued to fall into place for me during this wild and crazy adventure. Whenever I thought it could not possibly get any better, it did. I was filled with gratitude for my neighbor Frank. He really came through for me.

An hour later, I received the invitation. Everything I had focused on during the last year came together in the form of an actual golden ticket, delivered by e-mail. Even Chrissy got a little caught up in the exhilaration over attending the event. I was elated that she was excited about it, too. I knew we would have a fabulous time in Philadelphia, one that would be memorable. We would be sitting in the president of MGM's seats—how great is that?

I called all my friends and told them I was going to the premiere. Anyone who knew me also knew how much this meant to me. There was a good chance I'd be onscreen, and I wanted to see it for the first time, sitting in that audience at that event.

It didn't take me long to make the arrangements. I reserved a hotel room in Philly, requested a day off from work, picked out the right suit and tie, and asked my eldest of three sisters, Maria, to watch our girls. Once again, everything was coming together and another adventure back to Philadelphia was only days away.

I was so in tune with my positive thoughts that when December 18th finally arrived, every aspect of my daily life was working out. Chrissy and I planned to leave early that morning so we could arrive in plenty of time. I wanted to be one of the first people at the premiere so we wouldn't miss a thing. We usually fall behind schedule, but on that special day, we were perfect.

My sister arrived at our home right on time, and she was very excited for me. She knew how much energy I had invested in this endeavor. It was an exciting morning for everyone. I double-checked to make sure I had everything, and it was finally time to leave.

"See you later," I said to my daughters, which was tough because they wanted to come with us. They were too young to understand why we had to leave them home. I tried to explain that we only had two tickets, and that seemed to make it a little easier. I loaded up the car, and we were officially ready to leave. I thanked Maria for helping us with the kids.

"Whatever you do, don't burn the house down," I said, "and call us if you need anything." She didn't seem to appreciate that comment very much, but no way could she get mad at me at that particular moment.

Our drive to Philadelphia was smooth sailing until an hour into the ride. We received a frantic call from my sister looking for the fire code to our house alarm. She had placed pancakes in the microwave on high for three minutes instead of thirty seconds. The smoke detector was blaring and she couldn't shut it off. I just had to laugh. No doubt that was a tough phone call to make because I'm sure she knew I would never let her live that down. I was truly grateful that it was just a little smoke, along with some major embarrassment. We gave her the alarm code and told her to open the windows. It was quickly under control, and we laughed the rest of the way to Philadelphia. Everything seemed to be manifesting as planned, and I was in high spirits as we anticipated what lay ahead that night.

We arrived nice and early and checked into our hotel, giving us plenty of time to grab a quick lunch and get a little rest. We planned to leave the hotel around 4:30 p.m. Even though I had my car, we would take a cab to the theater so I wouldn't have to worry about parking.

This would be a night to remember for the rest of our lives. We were attending the gala premiere of *Rocky Balboa*; we had the best VIP seats in the house; and we would party the night away with the cast of stars. The only thing I was still anxious about was whether I would be seen in the movie. Would I get my one second of fame?

Finally it was time; we were looking good and ready for our big night. Chrissy suffered no wardrobe malfunctions, like a snag in her stockings or shoes that hurt her feet. Everything was perfect. I felt jubilant as we rode the elevator down to the lobby. The doorman hailed us a cab that was right there waiting for us. Then it was off to the Prince Theater on Chestnut Street, and in that moment, we felt like stars ourselves.

The hotel was close to the theater so we got there quickly, right around 5 p.m. as planned. The street was already crowded with traffic everywhere. Thousands of people were lined up behind police barriers, cheering wildly as guests arrived. Our cab pulled up in front of the theater, and when we stepped out onto the red carpet, it was a tremendous rush. This was about as cool as it could ever be. We stood there for awhile and soaked in everything that was going on. We were early, but quite a few people had already arrived.

"What should we do now?" I asked Chrissy.

"You might as well ask for our tickets."

Two nice girls were sitting at a table set up for the will call tickets with envelopes bearing people's names on them. This is it, I thought to myself. I'm going to get the president of MGM's tickets. I must confess that I felt like a big shot. I couldn't wait to say my name because I hoped they would know those were special seats just for us. I walked up to the table with all the confidence in the world and gave them my name. One girl looked at me and then flipped through the envelopes.

"Here you go, Mr. Cantatore. Enjoy the premiere."

That's all there was to it. Holding the tickets in my hand, I thought about that for the longest time. I remained positive this moment would happen. There was never the slightest doubt in my mind. Chrissy was looking at me with a gorgeous smile; she knew what it meant and was so happy for me.

I opened the envelope to inspect these great seats befitting a president. Chrissy was watching my face as my expression turned upside-down.

"What's wrong?" she asked.

"Mezzanine, Row R," I grumbled.

"What?"

"Mezzanine, Row R," I repeated. "They gave us Mezzanine, Row R, Seats 1 and 2."

"That's not possible," she said. "Maybe you should go back and ask if you got the right tickets."

"I can't embarrass myself by doing that."

I felt so deflated and started grousing. Then my wife did what she does best when I get carried away; she brought me right back.

"What are you so upset about?" she asked. "You're in. You have tickets to the premiere of *Rocky Balboa*, just like you always wanted and talked about forever." She told me to look at all the people standing behind the barriers, wishing they had my tickets. "Stop your bellyaching and be grateful for what you have. Let's go inside."

Chrissy put everything back into perspective for me, and she was right. I had no reason whatsoever to complain. I was officially at the premiere of *Rocky Balboa*, no matter where I sat. So I quickly got over my first disappointment of the night, and we headed in.

As only a handful of people were already inside the theater, I felt like we succeeded in our get-there-early mission. We stood around, not knowing what to do with ourselves. As more guests entered, the atmosphere became more exhilarating by the second. I stood there and did what I do best. I scanned the room and took mental notes on everything happening around me. The theater lobby was thronged with excited guests as it got closer to showtime.

My first celebrity sighting of the evening arrived in the person of ESPN radio host and HBO boxing analyst Max Kellerman. I acknowledged him by name and quoted a line from his radio show to indicate I was in his army. He knew right away that I was from New York. He shook my hand as we introduced ourselves. I mentioned that I was in the radio business as well, and we had a short conversation about the communications industry.

I then noticed my *Philadelphia Enquirer* friends, Michael and Tom from *Rocky Stories,* and walked over to say hello. I introduced them to Chrissy and thanked them for inviting me to their recent book release event. They, in turn, introduced me to a very tall man with grey hair they were hanging out with. He was Garrett Brown, the man who invented the Steadicam. He's an Academy Award winner and is acclaimed for his skillful work in filming steadily while running up the Rocky Steps. That turned out to be one of the greatest movie scenes of all time. I was thrilled to meet Garrett Brown in person. While speaking to him, I overheard Michael telling his wife about me. I had the impression that he appreciated my networking efforts. He knew how much I wanted to attend this event, and I think he was a little surprised to see me there. I wondered how much of a fan he was because he seemed to know a lot of good people involved in the films. I was proud to be in his company that night.

As it got closer to 7 p.m., the energy in the lobby was palpable. Before long, I could hear a buzz going on outside. I wondered what was happening out there, but I didn't want to lose my place inside. So Chrissy and I stayed next to the elevator door, and I continued to survey the room, checking out everyone and everything.

Two gentlemen walked by telling guests it was time to go inside the theater and find our seats because Mr. Stallone was entering the building. I was eager to see his entrance, but not excited to find my seat in Mezzanine, Row R. I stepped aside and that bought us some extra time in the lobby. As the crowd thinned out, Chrissy got to watch me in action again. She has been with me long enough to know what was coming next. I kept my eye on the prize.

Being a large guy dressed in a professional suit, I walked right up to one of the security guards, and without thinking, said, "Excuse me, sir. Please enter the theater now as Mr. Stallone will be making his entrance."

The security guard stared at me with a puzzled look on his face and stated that he was security. I apologized to him and said that I was security also. I then turned to the couple standing next to him and asked them to please enter the theater. The guard bought it and left us alone even when I told him Chrissy was with me.

The lobby was now clear, and we were the only ones there except for the other security guards. That's when I looked around and saw Sylvester Stallone entering the lobby with his family. I walked over to say hello and congratulated him on the movie premiere. And then—can you believe this—I escorted the guest of honor into the theater. I played the part seriously, but inside I was beaming. Chrissy knew exactly what I was up to, and she was tickled to see me pulling off this charade. I was actually walking Sylvester Stallone into the premiere of his own movie *Rocky Balboa;* talk about a successful moment.

It was time to find our seats. I had pushed my limits as far as possible without going overboard. As Stallone headed down to the stage, we climbed the stairs to the mezzanine. It was a packed house except for one row that was entirely empty: Mezzanine, Row R. I was trying to think of a logical reason as to why that was when I recognized Michael Vitez and his guests, including Garrett Brown, sitting in Row S right behind us. Of all possible seats in that entire theater, we were directly in front of them. I wondered how he ended up in the mezzanine too. I turned around and smiled at him with a nod and a wave. Knowing I was nervous about whether or not I would be in the actual movie, Michael leaned forward to wish me luck as the house lights went down.

I whispered to Chrissy how weird it was that we were the only two people in our row. At that time, Jimmy Binns, the lawyer guy, took the stage and introduced Sylvester Stallone, who came out with one of his young daughters. The audience went crazy and gave him a grand ovation. Sly addressed the crowd and explained his motivation for making the new sequel. He talked about doing anything you set your mind to, no matter how old you are—just another connection for me. After thanking all of the people involved in making the film a reality, he said, "I would now like to introduce you to the cast of *Rocky Balboa*."

He pointed over to the doors where I had walked him into the theater, and as we all looked to the right, in walked the cast, led by the friendliest face ever, Burt Young. The crowd gave them another great ovation as they waved and headed up the steps. I sat there mesmerized as the entire cast climbed into Mezzanine, Row R. They filled up our row, which was actually in perfect alignment with the large movie screen. I looked at Chrissy, and she saw my excitement return. Mezzanine, Row R, Seats 1 and 2 really did belong to the president of MGM after all, and we were sitting with the cast of *Rocky Balboa*. It was crazy, unbelievably crazy for me, a lifelong fan. I glanced over as they filled in the row and was surprised to see a familiar face from back home. Our former Nassau County Executive and fellow Long Islander, the Honorable Thomas Gulotta, was seated next to Burt Young. I filed the information away, knowing that somehow this connection could work to my advantage later on.

The MGM lion roared onscreen, and I thought to myself, I did it. Look at me now; here I am at the premiere. Who would ever believe this amazing story? After a year of endless effort, this incredible journey was manifesting right before my eyes. But my contentment came to an abrupt end as the movie started and I began to fret all over again whether I would be seen in it or not.

A new version of the famous song "Take You Back" played, and the movie was on. The first scene featured Mason Dixon fighting at the Mandalay Bay in a cold, dark setting with a black and white effect. My eyes fixated on the ringside front row, and I recognized half a dozen extras that I hung out with back in Vegas. The scene was shot on one of the two days that I missed on-set, so now I was getting nervous that I had missed out completely. I squirmed with anticipation waiting for the fight scene. I have to admit, that as much as I enjoyed the movie, I was mostly preoccupied with thoughts about that fight scene.

The storyline followed the traditional formula, with everything you would expect from a *Rocky* film. The flashback scenes really affected me, taking me back to the first time I saw the movie when I was a kid.

Paulie put everything into perspective when he told his friend Rocco that he was living in the past, and he couldn't do it anymore. I watched Paulie on the big screen, and then I looked down my row at Burt Young—it was an incredible moment. I remembered that day at the diner when I was twelve years old and he had treated me so well. A lot of my passion for *Rocky* stems from that day. On this night, however, I appreciated Mr. Young, not only for his portrayal of Paulie, but for the man himself. Turning my attention to the screen once again, I took in the footage of Philadelphia. Everything about the city was still fresh in my head from the many trips I'd taken there during the last year.

The rest of the movie flowed nicely, setting itself up for the big fight scene at the end. It was now time to see if I had made the cut. I wanted the suspense to end. I needed to know that "I did it," that I would receive my flash-second of fame.

Finally, it was happening. Initially I expected to see myself with the entrance of the fighters, and I prepared to scan the crowd of extras. The HBO graphics gave the scene a real-life boxing effect. The cameras then panned to the announcers. I was sitting behind them when they shot the scene, but I couldn't see myself. Then the fighters arrived, and this was it—my eyes popped wide open. As Rocky and his team entered the ring to a familiar Frank Sinatra song, "High Hopes," everything looked different to me. None of the familiar extras were appearing on the screen, including me. I was confused. (I later found out that the entrance scene in the movie had been shot during an actual boxing match the night before the filming that I attended. Stallone wanted the authentic effect of a real crowd in a packed house.) I was confused by the switch because this should have been my big scene. I had anticipated the possibility of disappointment because this was Hollywood, after all, and that's the breaks in show biz.

First, I had to get my bearings straight and find my corner of the ring. This distracted me from watching the movie; I just searched the crowd for familiar faces. I recognized a bunch of people I had met a year earlier, but not me. My disappointment deepened.

Toward the middle of the second round, the action got dramatic when Rocky was knocked down for a second time in the fight, and the devastating blow happened right in front of me in the corner of the ring where I was seated. I had devoured every second of this exchange as it happened live in Las Vegas, and now it was playing out again on the giant screen. I perked up, knowing this had to be it. This was the point during the filming where I leapt to my feet, yelling at Rocky to get up. The camera panned from Rocky staggering on the mat, over to Paulie shouting at him, and back to Rocky. And then it happened—my big Italian face flashed on the screen!

I squeezed Chrissy's hand as we savored that moment. It was all I could do to keep from shouting "I did it!" A lifelong dream had been realized. I was in the *Rocky Balboa* movie. That first glimpse opened a new dimension that I can only describe as awesome. My energy was zinging in every direction. Now that I knew exactly where I appeared in the film, the pressure was off, and I spotted myself a few more times after that. However, I still didn't see much of the fight scene because I continued to watch for familiar faces. Since I was the first one to see the movie, I couldn't wait to e-mail some of my new friends to tell them how great it was.

And then, just like that, it was over—The End—and the house lights came on. Michael, sitting behind me, bent forward to say congratulations, confirming he had seen me. Glowing with gratification, I thanked him, but my mind was already planning my next goal: mixing with the cast members. I looked down our row as the actors filed out, and I probably climbed over a few people to reach Mr. Gulotta, the well-known former politician from Long Island.

"So what is Nassau County's best county executive doing in Philadelphia?" I inquired.

Chrissy stood clear as I reintroduced myself to Mr. Gulotta, whom I had met numerous times over the years. I reminded him that I was from the *Long Island Press* and shook his hand. Once again, I had networked with the right person.

As the crowd spilled out into the main lobby, I stayed close to Tom, and he personally introduced me to Burt, who looked at me like he knew me. For the fourth time in my life, I reminded him of our connection and thanked him for his kindness to me in Las Vegas. I asked Burt if I could to take a photo with him and Tom, but I had to laugh when he pushed me aside and grabbed Chrissy instead. That accomplished, he did consent to take that photo with me and Mr. Gulotta.

I rarely get star struck, but this glorious night was different, and I relished every moment. I have never cared about autographs, but I do enjoy photos, and on this special night, my goal was to take my picture with everyone. I wanted to remember everything on film. After the picture with Burt in the lobby, I took one with Jimmy Binns. Chrissy and I then dashed outside to catch a cab because I sure didn't want to miss a second of that exclusive afterparty.

During our short ride over to the Philadelphia Museum of Art, I teased Chrissy about her photo op with Burt, and we laughed again at how he shoved me out of the way. She clearly enjoyed his flirtatious attention. The next experience was moments away and I marveled how the whole night was working out perfectly. We knew that with our positive thought process even more excitement awaited us, including another meeting with the star of the film. The next round would even include an astonishing spiritual connection all brought on by a continued belief in the Rocky Spirit.

ROUND TWELVE

Defining an Orb

It was official, I made the final cut and it was time to celebrate the accomplishment. As the cab pulled up to the museum, we anticipated a big night out at this special location. Chrissy took a few great shots of me walking up the steps, but this time we weren't stopping at the top. We were going inside the Philadelphia Museum of Art to party with the cast of *Rocky Balboa*.

For all the many times I had visited these famous steps, I had never entered this world-class museum. This night was different. I took a deep breath, slowly opened the front doors and entered the magnificent lobby. It was my first Hollywood premiere, and I was about to mingle with the stars.

Once inside the main room, I noticed Sylvester Stallone standing in the middle of a crowd. On a wall right behind him there was an art exhibit of a towering gold crucifix. For some reason, my mind flashed back to the opening scene of the original film at the old church. It symbolized that God was watching over Rocky, as if he were the Chosen One. Was this moment a simple coincidence, or evidence of a divine presence?

The lively party was already in full swing, and Sly was surrounded by a throng of admiring guests. They besieged him with requests for photos and autographs. A second photograph was another goal of mine, but timing is everything. I waited patiently for the opportune chance.

I circulated and networked with most of the cast members, being ever so careful not to intrude on anyone's privacy or appear overbearing. I just wanted to fit in. We hung out with Burt again and had another conversation with HBO commentator Max Kellerman about the movie, his role in it, boxing and more. Max was a cool guy; he even impressed Chrissy.

I continued to work the room, memorizing every detail of this splendid affair. We took pictures with everybody, including actress Geraldine Hughes and Sly's wife Jennifer Flavin. I approached her as the crowd was mobbing her husband and, with what I hoped was an engaging smile, I asked if I could take a picture with her. Her answer surprised me.

"No, thank you," she replied, turning away.

She must have thought I was some creep trying to take her photo. I smiled again and explained that I was a dad who had young daughters, just like her.

"In fact, that's my wife with the camera," I said, pointing over to Chrissy. "She'll take the picture."

Jennifer looked beyond me to acknowledge her with a smile and a wave. She extended her hand to greet Chrissy.

"Is this your husband?" she asked.

"I don't like to admit it, but yes, he really is with me."

They shared a laugh at my expense, and then she gave me permission to take the picture. It was a classic exchange, and I certainly respected her initial reaction. Jennifer Flavin proved to be a classy supermodel.

I then found myself standing right next to Sly. Here was my second opportunity in three months to take a photo with him. We posed together and also shook hands. Wanting to be professional, I quickly stepped aside afterward. I'd had my moment.

We walked away and strolled around, stopping to admire a unique flight of slate steps inside the museum. Chrissy suggested I stand on them for another cool photo op. As she clicked away, I noticed Frank Stallone striding across the room straight toward me.

"What did you think about my remake of 'Take You Back'?" he asked.

I must admit that I felt honored when he acknowledged me the way he did and asked my opinion. I told him honestly that it was great and I had enjoyed it. It was a new, upbeat version of the song and a perfect way to begin the movie. I continued to engage him in conversation and seized the moment to share the details of my "Run-the-Rocky-Steps" promotion. I even showed him the center spread in the *Long Island Press* and my cover story. I had these few pages of the newspaper folded up in the pocket of my suit jacket, just waiting for the right opportunity. It was one of those nights—I held the dice and was rolling nothing but sevens. If I were writing a script of my experience, I could not have imagined anything as perfect as this.

After visiting with Frank, Chrissy and I met with Burt one last time to thank him. He introduced us to a lady friend of his who was also from Long Island, and we knew some of the same people from back home. Was this another so-called coincidence in my *Rocky* saga?

We talked shop some more with Max, and by the time we finished, most of the crowd had thinned out. The two of us continued to wander around, speaking to anyone who still lingered. We ran into a friendly woman who worked as a hostess at the Victor Café, the real establishment that doubled as Adrian's Restaurant in the movie. She shared with us that Stallone personally picked her husband to play the role of a bar thug. I knew who she was referring to; Rocky had manhandled him outside the bar in the film. I told her that I thought he had played the part well and asked if he was at the party in order to meet him. I was shocked to learn her husband had passed away unexpectedly during the year and never got the chance to see his screen debut. That solemn exchange put life into perspective and plunged me back down to Earth.

The young lady was thinking positively, however, believing that her husband joined her that night in spirit. I agreed and think about that moment every time I see him in the movie. Life certainly has many surprising twists and turns. We spent a little more time with the young widow and shared some laughs to change the somber mood.

By then we realized that we were about the only people left besides the waitstaff. It had been a long and wonderful day. The party was over, but something about that moment filled me with energy.

I recall scanning the gallery one last time to see if anyone else was still around, but it was officially empty. I found myself gazing at the gold crucifix. Again, it reminded me of the beginning of the Italian Stallion's journey. The exhibit was a rood screen from an old church dating back to 1783. It was part of the Tesoros/Treasures/Tesouros collection. This fascinating crucifix radiated with energy. For some unexplained reason, it seemed to make perfect sense regarding the spiritual energy that was surrounding me. As I continued to focus on the crucifix, I thanked God for this amazing experience.

Chrissy caught my attention with a loving smile and asked in a soft voice, "Are you done?"

This was the same part of my story that I began to detail in Round One. It has now caught up and gone full circle to clarify the meaning of that mysterious flash of bright light. This epiphany would allow me to understand my place in the universe and mission from God.

I turned to look at her and smiled back with a blank stare.

"Are you done?" she repeated.

"Yeah, I'm done," I said. "Let's go."

I understood what she meant by that. I took some time to appreciate the moment and reflect on everything I had accomplished over my lifetime as a

Rocky fan, with added focus on the last few years. *I did it.* Up until this point, it was a remarkable journey. A dream became a reality that night and I had to overcome some obstacles in order to go the distance.

We exited the museum and walked out onto the expansive patio that opens to the top of the famous Rocky Steps overlooking the city. It was this magnificent view that inspired one more idea. I asked Chrissy if she would take one final photograph of me from behind raising my arm in victory. I was highly charged and still sizzling with energy and gratitude. I knew it was impossible that the camera broke when my wife took the initial photograph but I remained curious about the large flash of light that startled her. I was unaware of what would become of it.

When we arrived home the following afternoon, I went straight to the office and Chrissy got some much-needed rest. That evening, I couldn't wait to download the images from the camera to our computer, though, I was not prepared for the spiritual experience that was about to redirect my course.

Each photo would be a cherished memory of that star-studded premiere. On the third-to-last picture, the one that Chrissy said broke the camera; I saw something startling that gave me the chills. On that photograph, a giant, mysterious circle of light appeared to emanate from my raised fist. It was way too big to be the moon and the sky was clear when we took the picture, so what was it?

I studied the image, trying to figure out an explanation for this anomaly. Sometimes in photographs, you can see small, cloud-like circles called orbs, but this was not small. It was enormous, and certainly the most astonishing orb I'd ever seen. I believed it to be spiritual energy, something very special, which sent another round of tingles zinging through my body.

This circle of energy was perfect and powerful in every way. My heart rate accelerated when I enlarged the image of the orb to look more closely at the many molecules of different colored particles inside. They seemed to move about on the screen and began to play tricks on my eyes. I shouted to Chrissy to come downstairs and take a look. She hurried to see what all the excitement was about.

Before she had a chance to look, I asked her, "What exactly happened last night when you saw that big flash of white light on the camera screen, when you thought the camera broke?"

She described a large, unexplainable flash of light that popped on the screen and startled her, causing her to jump back.

"Okay," I said, "brace yourself and take a look at what you photographed."

Her jaw dropped in amazement when she saw the photo with the giant, perfect circle of energy. The astonished look on her face confirmed that it was something special.

"What is that?" she asked.

"I think it's an orb," I said.

"Are you kidding me?"

"I think it's a message from above."

Chrissy knew what I meant. She has experienced a few inexplicable spiritual moments with me throughout the years, enough to have her believing in the power of faith and this orb.

It made me think about my father, and I turned around to smile at his picture on the wall behind me. Returning my attention to the computer, I felt that this extraordinary photograph marked a perfect ending. In my heart, mind, and soul, this image of spiritual energy justified my unique journey and passion to be a part of the *Rocky* saga. There was a reason, after all, why I related so strongly to those films. But it was not an ending in a strange twist, the photograph turned out to be the beginning to the later rounds of my story.

The energy orb has led me on a new path of awareness about my faith, trust in God and my belief in the Holy Trinity. By asking for guidance through prayer, many great things may happen as you climb the ladder of personal success. Throughout the series, Rocky connected with the same spiritual energy. One thing I knew for sure, the orb was a sign urging me to share my own million-to-one experience with others as motivation to seek their own faith and goals in life.

ROUND THIRTEEN
Confirming a Universal Law

In the days and months that followed, I shared my photograph of the mystifying image with many people, some who were "in the cosmic know," and others who just thought it was a great shot of the moon. After I described how it originated, including all the ironies of my story, the orb elicited a new meaning from each person. I enjoyed watching their expressions when they heard the details behind the unique photograph. Almost every person would say, "I just got a chill."

After seeing the orb for the first time, I became aware of how its spiritual power linked with my *Rocky* experiences. I was always in the right place, or received perfectly timed information from unlikely sources that led me to another connection. I knew something even bigger was coming down the road, as I kept running into opportunities to interact with members of the *Rocky* family.

In early March 2007, I once again met up with Talia Shire and revisited a favorite childhood memory. The popular actress was starring in a live reading of a play called *Agnes of God* at a local college theater. A friend, who connected me with *Rocky*, told me about the performance at the last minute. I decided to swing by the theater to request a press photo of Ms. Shire before the show began. I grabbed Pete and we headed over, bringing along a copy of the *Long Island Press* that featured my cover story.

We arrived early to snap a quick photograph and keep out of the way.

Once inside though, I met the director of the production who suggested that we stay for the entire performance. We could take the picture at the end, and he would introduce us to her.

I couldn't wait to meet this beautiful woman again and tell her that one of my favorite childhood memories was the day she kissed me on the cheek. After the show, Pete and I were brought backstage and reintroduced to Ms. Shire. We asked her a few questions about the play and the latest *Rocky* film. Pete asked if she was disappointed that her character, Adrian, died in the sixth movie. She explained that Stallone, the writer and director, had consulted with her about the decision to eliminate her famed role in the last sequel.

"I love Stallone," she said, "and that decision was the right thing to do."

She also told us how the timing of her character's passing paralleled her own personal situation regarding the recent loss of her husband. It seemed like yet another spiritual connection. I believed there was an important reason that we had the chance to ask the same question to the actress that we had asked the actor. Both were affected by this storyline in the *Rocky Balboa* sequel. I knew it was related to my journey.

To change the mood of the conversation, I handed her a copy of the newspaper and mentioned the part about our first meeting when she kissed me on the cheek. Thirty years later, I still remembered that wonderful moment as if it had happened only yesterday. A beautiful smile spread across her face, and much to my surprise, Ms. Shire took my hand, looked at me, and said, "Thank you." She then leaned forward and kissed me again on that very same cheek. I was twelve years old all over again. Talia Shire, the magnificent actress who played Adrian Balboa, had just bestowed a second kiss on my cheek, and even as a grown man, I was blushing.

A few months later, I had another chance meeting with Frank Stallone. Pete had taken me to the Chiller Theater Convention at a hotel in New Jersey as guests of a friend who was promoting the show. The convention featured some great, familiar faces from television and Hollywood. It wasn't until we arrived that we learned one of the celebrity guests was Frank Stallone. We would meet up with him once again.

Frank's table was bustling with a continuous crowd of fans seeking autographs. When the demand on him eased up a bit, I saw my opportunity to stop by and greet him. At first, he gave me that I-know-you look again, but after a brief reminder, he did remember me, and we engaged in conversation.

He told me about his role in a new movie called *Fred Claus* that was coming out for the holiday season. I reminded him that I was in the media business, and my company owned radio stations and a newspaper. Frank said he might get in touch with me to set up a radio interview to promote the movie.

"Sure, contact me anytime," I said, and handed him my business card. As I walked away, I thought how cool it would be to help him with the interview.

A month later around the end of November, an e-mail popped up on my Outlook—from Frank Stallone. It was an eCard wishing me a Merry Christmas! I was happy that he remembered me and replied immediately, returning the greeting. Moments later he wrote back to ask if I would be interested in arranging that radio interview to promote his movie. Naturally, I was happy to make it happen, and eventually we worked out all the details. Once again, I was getting more connected to the *Rocky* universe, and wondered if the orb had something to do with it.

So many connections, both large and small, continued to unfold and were *Rocky*-related. They occurred with new people I met or through simple conversations with others along the way. Some associations were directly related to the orb.

In April 2008, I was chosen to be an honoree at an event for the Center of Hope at a local children's hospital. I felt spiritually connected to this organization. They help families, especially children, cope with the death of a loved one. At their gala, I gave a heartfelt speech about my own personal experience with the loss of my father.

In the pocket of my suit jacket, I carried two photographs close to my heart; one of my dad and another of the orb. The picture of my father was a smaller version of the same one I had turned around to look at immediately after seeing the orb for the first time on my computer screen. After delivering an emotional speech at the event, I approached my friend and personally invited guest, Marcy Neumann, who founded a self-help company called Heartlites Incorporated. Her business promotes the art of positive thinking and the Law of Attraction. Marcy is a wonderful person in every way, and I am fortunate to be her friend. She understands spiritual energy through her work with clients and many of her own life experiences.

She complimented me on my speech, saying she connected with me through my emotional spirit. That prompted me to ask if she knew anything about energy orbs.

"Yes, sure I do," she replied, in a sweet tone.

Marcy was enthusiastic and curious when I offered to show her the amazing photograph. I removed the picture from my pocket and flipped it over. She recognized immediately what it was and its significance, especially after just having heard my speech.

Marcy studied it, and I could tell she was intrigued. Her jaw dropped and her mouth fell open, just like others who had viewed it before her. I told her there was a story behind it, and she insisted we get together so she could hear about it. We made a significant connection through the impact of this unique energy orb.

I met her for breakfast at a diner the following week to share my story in complete detail. She then confirmed her belief that the orb represents pure spiritual energy. That very morning, she urged me to write this book. Marcy believed the orb was a sign that my story needed to be told for some significant reason. She said that I was being called on by the universe to share it.

"Marcy, I really don't think I have a book in me," I protested.

"*Think again*," she said.

My thoughts drifted back to the cover story I had written two years earlier. I actually won the 2007 Press Club of Long Island (PCLI) journalism award for best arts story, even though I wasn't a professional writer. I considered that a one-time thing and wasn't prepared to embark on a new project; but Marcy knew exactly what needed to happen. She believed this was my calling, and she had a plan to get me started.

Toward the end of 2008, Marcy invited me as a guest speaker to tell my story at one of her seminars on the power of positive thinking, goal setting and the Law of Attraction. I jumped at the opportunity to talk before a live audience and joined her as a guest speaker. Marcy Neumann eventually became a mentor and helped awaken my spiritual awareness.

I intended to tell what I thought would be a simple *Rocky* story and close by showing my photograph of the amazing energy orb. However, as I approached the podium that afternoon, a flood of unexplainable knowledge and awareness came over me that was simply magical. My mind and thought process had been stimulated during Marcy's seminar, and I began to comprehend why I had been invited that day. I realized that my saga was not just about a young man's passion for his all-time favorite movie, it was a spiritual story about a life journey that was manifested through the Law of Attraction and a belief in spiritual energy.

I stood in front of a room filled with people, still not sure what I was going to say. Without a script in hand, I began to speak from my heart. I could feel the powerful words effortlessly flowing out of me, especially as I addressed the Law of Attraction and its connection to my story. Up until that moment, I never really understood this universal principle. I'm not even sure where the words came from that day, as they just poured out of me.

At the conclusion of my portion of the seminar, I showed the mystical photograph on a large screen. The audience sat with mouths agape, amazed by the image itself and the significance of the mysterious orb. They understood it and got it as we were all like-minded. Afterward, a dozen people approached me and confirmed Marcy's assertion that I should write a book. They urged me to share the story with others because my experience had happened for a reason. I should make it my mission in life to perpetuate this story and allow it to make a difference in the lives of others. I now fully understood why Marcy invited me to speak that day, and I am forever grateful for her encouragement to share this story.

My journey was manifesting quickly with the help of a powerful spiritual message that others were encouraging me to share. I pondered what to do next. Now with a better understanding of the Law of Attraction, I was curious where it would take me. I knew that someday I would find the impetus to put this story down on paper, even as more interesting connections and coincidences continued to happen.

Shortly after the seminar, I ran into Burt again at an Italian restaurant on Long Island called Vincent's Clam Bar. I had stopped in one night to visit one of the owners named Bobby who is a client and friend of mine. He was aware of my unusual *Rocky* connections from prior conversations. That evening, he said that he had a little surprise for me and told me to look over at the corner table. It was none other than Burt Young enjoying dinner with the same lady that I had met at the premiere back in Philadelphia. Moments later, Bobby walked me over for yet another introduction to the actor. When Burt and his companion looked up, they recognized my by-now familiar face, but out of context, he couldn't quite place me. I explained myself again, and we had a pleasant conversation. When Burt asked how I knew Bobby, I reminded him about the *Long Island Press* and gave him my business card. He mentioned an art expo that he was hosting at a nearby library. Burt said he would invite me and I was excited about the opportunity.

A few weeks later, as promised, an invitation to the opening night of the art exhibit featuring Burt's paintings arrived. So Pete got that call again and we set out for another *Rocky* connection. It was interesting that in the latest movie, Paulie had been portrayed as a painter, and now I saw firsthand how Hollywood paired the character's interests with the actor's real-life talents.

Pete and I grabbed a few moments to speak with Burt and share some laughs with him. Since I knew he had a connection to Long Island, I asked if we might break bread together someday. He said yes and told me to arrange it through his friend. I followed through with a few e-mails, but we could never put anything together because of Burt's busy schedule. I was convinced, however, that I would meet up with him again because things happen, and don't happen, for a reason. I knew that an opportunity would manifest itself down the road.

A few months later, in what seemed like an unrelated incident at the time, the Orlando Chamber of Commerce in Florida invited me to come speak about a successful discount card program I had helped develop for my company. A former coworker of mine had recently moved to Orlando. While attending a chamber meeting there, he learned of their plans to launch an identical program to the one we had been using for the last year. He told them of my role in the development of this program and recommended they bring me down as their guest speaker for the event. When I arrived in Orlando, I was struck by the fact that they had designed an exact replica of our program, and yet we knew nothing about each other. It was clearly another Law-of-Attraction experience.

I took the podium that day with a prepared speech in hand, but quickly went off topic. I mentioned a book called *The Secret*, even though I had not read it or seen the video. But I did know that it explained the power of the Law of Attraction, which we were currently experiencing. I told the audience we had two programs that were identical in every way, that were created in two different states, with no communication or interaction. That was enough to convince me to buy the DVD of *The Secret* and learn more about the concept.

The next Sunday afternoon, I settled into my favorite seat on the couch and began to watch it. The video featured an interview with Jack Canfield. I had never heard of him before, but I learned that he was the author of a bestseller called *Chicken Soup for the Soul* and a number of similar titles related to the original. He talked about writing his famous book and how a series of connections led him to achieve his goal of publishing it and the others that followed.

As I watched the interview, I thought about Marcy urging me to write a book about my *Rocky* experience. At that exact moment, I got up and walked over to the computer. I sat down and typed a title and drafted my first paragraph. I then returned to the couch to finish watching the DVD. My mission to share this story was born on a Sunday afternoon in May 2009.

The agony of trying to write that first chapter was excruciating. I was getting nowhere. One weekend, I fell asleep around midnight, but woke up at 2 a.m. with an incredible burst of energy. My mind was a jumble of thoughts; a deluge of words was reaching flood stage, and I had no idea where this was coming from. I jumped out of bed and spent the next eight hours at the computer, organizing the outline of my book.

It took me four months to complete the first draft, and I rewrote parts of it many times over the next few years. Somehow I assumed that my Rocky story had a beginning and an end, but in truth, it turned out to be an ongoing journey with many surprises ahead.

I was elated upon the completion of the first draft of the book in August 2009. I thought it would be cool to share my story with Burt someday, but I never wanted to be pushy about meeting up with him.

That same month, a client invited me to a golf tournament in support of the American Kidney Fund. The charity was honoring former Nassau County Executive Thomas Gulotta. He was my Long Island connection at the premiere in Philadelphia. I was already planning to attend the golf outing, but now that I knew who would be there, I was on a mission. I approached Mr. Gulotta at the event and reintroduced myself. When he asked what I was up to these days, it opened the door for me to tell him about my book. I said that I was hoping to meet up with Burt again in order to share my story with him. Mr. Gulotta asked for my business card and suggested I write the word "book" on the back to remind him about our conversation. He said he would contact Burt on my behalf.

About two weeks later, Mr. Gulotta called and asked if I would post some pictures and a press release about the charity event on our publication's Web site. He then invited me to lunch and asked me to bring along a copy of the book. I met him at a local Italian restaurant and shared a mini version of my story with him, including the photograph of the orb. I was honored when he said that he loved it and would contact Burt for me to arrange a meeting.

The very next day, I received a telephone call from a familiar voice—Burt Young. He said if Tom Gulotta suggested that he meet with someone, then he knew he better do so. Burt was aware of my book and said he was interested in hearing about my story. We arranged a lunch meeting at a restaurant near his studio loft. I was thrilled about this opportunity and figured that he might give me an hour of his time and then try to get rid of me. I wondered what we would talk about and still could not believe that he was living on Long Island.

I met Burt at his loft, and he showed me all his fabulous paintings. Then we sat down to talk about some of our many connections, including that old carpet story. Before getting into the book, we decided to head over to a nearby restaurant for lunch. He grabbed my arm to walk me across the busy street, and I couldn't help wondering if anyone would recognize him. I could imagine them asking, "Who's that guy walking with Paulie?"

Once inside the restaurant, we were given the celebrity treatment, and I was feeling good. As we settled in, I pulled out the original manuscript and asked Burt if he believed in spiritual energy. I then proceeded to tell him about the story and showed him some photographs. He was curious to thumb through the draft. As I pointed out some passages, he went on to read a few extra pages on his own. Afterward, he said that my vision made me a part of the *Rocky* saga. Burt asked to borrow my pen and then wrote a few lines on his paper placemat. He said I could use his words in the book. I asked if he wanted to read the entire story.

"I don't have to," he replied. "I already know every word in this book. It's a masterpiece."

I smiled hearing those words. We finished our lunch and carried on about life and the *Rocky* movies. What I expected would be an hour-long conversation actually turned into a marathon of more than three hours. Finally, Burt said, "You gotta get back to work, kid? Get outta here."

And so ended one of the best lunch meetings of all time—I had made friends with Burt Young and now was certain that my book project had me on the right path toward the meaning of my journey.

Every connection I made advanced me closer to the goal of completing my story, but past experience suggested that I wasn't there yet. I sensed there would be one or two more chapters in my life that would get me to the Final Round in order to go the distance. The question was: Which direction would it take me?

In November 2009, I planned to attend an annual fundraiser on Long Island called Fight for Charity. This boxing exposition had been organized years earlier by a group of friends and business associates. One of the celebrity boxing judges at this year's event was to be former Heavyweight Champion of the World, Buster Douglas. In 1990, he shocked the universe in Tokyo, Japan with his famous knockout of the most-feared fighter in the world, the once-invincible Iron Mike Tyson. Buster had lived his own real-life *Rocky* story by having to overcome some major obstacles in order to win that fight and the title, including the death of this mother. I wanted to meet this spiritually unique individual.

The promoters usually bring in media people, such as newspaper publishers or reporters, to serve as unofficial judges alongside the celebrities. They had invited Jed, the publisher of my newspaper, but he was unable to attend, so he suggested they call me to work in his place. I loved the sport of boxing and jumped at the chance to be part of the action.

When I arrived at the hotel for the event, I was invited into the judges' suite for pre-fight cocktails. Within five minutes, Buster Douglas walked in, I couldn't believe the excellent timing. All I could focus on was the overwhelming size of this man's hand as I greeted him. It was easily twice as big as mine, which is fairly large to begin with. We barely had a chance to speak before the promoters ushered him away to meet others. I was pleased that my one mission of the night, to meet this guy, happened early on, but I was disappointed I didn't get to ask him about that legendary evening in Tokyo. I hoped I'd get another chance later that night.

I was escorted to the judges' table at ringside, and it was the closest I had been to a boxing event since the filming of *Rocky Balboa* back in Las Vegas. When I sat down, I noticed my nameplate in front of my seat. To the left was Buster Douglas. Not only would I get to meet the man again, but he would be sitting next to me for the entire night. I was extremely excited when the champ sat beside me. Surely this was meant to be part of my journey.

After a lot of small talk, I finally brought up Tokyo. It had been reported that his mother, Lula Pearl, had passed away just twenty-three days before the big fight. I asked Buster if he had felt her presence and spirit in the ring with him that night. With a wistful smile, he said that his mother was sitting squarely on his shoulder, and her spirit inspired him to achieve the near-impossible feat of winning the heavyweight title. He believed in himself through the spirit of his mom, and it was because of her energy that he stunned the world with his upset victory. Little did I imagine that this chance opportunity would eventually show me the way to complete my journey.

As I sat ringside watching some of my friends and business associates box in front of a large crowd of people, I wondered what it would be like to enter the boxing ring as a fighter myself. I considered it for a moment, but knew it would probably never happen. Training to be a charity boxer takes an inordinate amount of time and dedication, not only to get in shape to fight for three rounds, but also to do the fundraising. I quickly dismissed the notion, but remained curious the rest of the night. Later, I inquired about it when I spoke to one of the corner men, Ray Bettinelli, who owned the BCBA boxing gym. I always wanted to join a real boxing gym and train like a fighter. Ray said that his not-for-profit location was open to local kids for free, and adults could train there for minimal monthly dues. He suggested I come down to check it out sometime. That would be ideal, but I knew I wouldn't have the time.

When the event was over, I couldn't wait to step into the ring to bounce up and down and experience, however briefly, what it feels like to be a boxer. On doing so, I subconsciously set in motion the circumstances that would direct me to the end of my journey as a charity boxer the following year.

As I was leaving, I thanked the event founders Jeff, Jamie and Matt, the limo guy who had supplied the famous bus for my Rocky Steps promotion years earlier. I told them how much fun the night had been and that I secretly wished I could participate in the event as a boxer. Why were they all smiling at me? I picked up my judge's trophy and departed, with plenty of boxing thoughts bouncing around in my mind.

For some crazy reason, a week later I purchased a speed bag, a heavy bag and a stand at Modell's Sporting Goods. The package was featured in a Black Friday circular inside our newspaper, and the deal seemed too good to pass up. The only problem was that I didn't have any room for the equipment, so I stored the purchase in its original box in my garage. I never even opened it.

One of my goals for 2010 was to finish this book, but I seemed to be stalled for some reason. Something was missing. Was there yet another chapter waiting to be experienced? In February, Burt agreed to do me a favor by appearing as our celebrity guest for the annual Best of Long Island awards celebration that I was hosting for the newspaper. At the event, I reintroduced him to my wife. My children and sister Doreen got to meet him for the first time. Gina Marie and Adriana were excited to meet the famous actor and have their picture taken with him. I also introduced him to Matt the limo guy, which led to another connection later in the year.

Throughout the next few months, I continued to edit the manuscript numerous times, sharing it with a few people that I thought could help put it into final form. But for some reason, I always hit a wall, ran into roadblocks, or heard different opinions on how to tell the story. I finally stopped making edits and left it untouched for a long period of time.

One day, I confided to Pete that I was stuck and didn't know where to take the project. We chatted about a few things, including some of the characters and actors in the *Rocky* movies. Pete is an avid memorabilia collector. A part of his hobby is searching the Internet for contact information on movie and television celebrities in an attempt to acquire autographs. He mentioned that he had come across a Web site posted by a cast member from the original *Rocky*.

He was speaking about Jimmy Gambina, the actor who played Mike the trainer from Mighty Mick's Gym and worked the corner during the fight scenes. Pete suggested I check out his Web site because it listed Gambina's contact information. I told him that four years ago, one of our staff reporters, a guy named Tom, had reached out to Gambina about doing a story on him. Tom said that Gambina was an interesting person who had a different perspective on the *Rocky* phenomena. I told Pete I would take a look, but didn't see how it would help my book project. I thought about researching it, but just filed it away in the back of my mind.

Weeks passed until one Saturday afternoon while surfing the Internet, I Googled Gambina's name and found his Web site. The first thing that jumped out at me was a link to the *Long Island Press* story, prominently displayed on the front page. There were also interesting photographs, and of course, Gambina's contact information, just like Pete had said. I stared at the screen and debated about placing a telephone call to him, and decided against it. I didn't want to just randomly call someone, so I closed the Web site and moved on. Maybe I would reach out to him someday.

Back at work on Monday morning, I checked my voicemail and listened to a message transferred to me by another Tom, our distribution manager. He introduced it by saying, "Felice, this message has to be for you; I have no idea how it came to me." Then the recording began. "Hey Tom, Jimmy Gambina from *Rocky*, we spoke awhile back. I'm just touching base with you to see how you're doing. Call me back when you get a chance."

It was a strange moment for me, almost like a psychic intervention. I had just researched this guy two days earlier and thought about contacting him, and now here was a message from him on my telephone. The call originally went to the wrong Tom because the reporter Gambina was trying to reach no longer worked with us. In a roundabout way, for whatever reason, I believe

I was meant to contact Jimmy Gambina after all. I just knew that he would somehow play an important role in my journey.

Later that night, I placed a call to Jimmy at his home in California, explaining who I was and the unusual connection between us. We had a great conversation about my book project, the *Rocky* movies, and his training experiences with Sylvester Stallone. Jimmy advised me that if I was going to write a book, I should know the truth about the Rocky phenomena. We talked for an hour, and he filled my head with plenty of information. I asked Jimmy if I could keep in touch with him. He replied that I sounded sincere and knowledgeable, and he believed there was some cosmic reason that we connected with each other. After the call, I stored his home telephone number in my cell phone address book under the name Jimmy, Mike from *Rocky*.

Over the next few weeks, I contacted him several times to discuss a lot of different things, including boxing, Rocky, and God. Jimmy has a strong religious faith and a true love for boxing; he cares about the reputation of the sport. During one of our conversations, he gave me a homework assignment. He said I needed to watch two movies about boxing: one called *The Champ*, which I was familiar with, and *Black Cloud*. Actor Ricky Schroeder and Gambina were involved with both films. He instructed me to call him back after I watched the two movies.

I purchased both films, knowing that we would have many more discussions in the future. I took away one important lesson from our first conversation: Never just blindly accept anything as the truth in Hollywood or in boxing—always learn all the facts. If I was going to write a book, I needed to know more about the *Rocky* franchise and the people involved. I had the sense that this was indeed happening for a reason. It was—to give me clarity that would help me get to the finish line.

I began to realize there was much more to my story, and would now be seeing things from a different perspective. I kept in touch with Jimmy and enjoyed discussing the movies with him. I gained new insight into boxing from a guy who had associated with some of the greats.

My journey continued to unfold when Jeff one of the Fight for Charity founders called me in May. I assumed he wanted me to be a judge again for the 2010 event coming up in November. He said he had talked to Matt, the owner of the limousine company, who told him about my *Rocky* and Burt Young connection.

I had run into Matt a month earlier at an expo and brought him up to date on my story and my recent interactions with Burt. We discussed the possibility of landing him as a celebrity boxing judge. Then Matt went so far as to suggest that I volunteer to fight as a charity boxer. I admit that the idea of participating in the event had been percolating in my mind for several months, but my busy schedule did not allow enough time to train. I told him there was no way I could participate.

When Jeff called me, he said Matt had recommended that I step into the ring for the charity match. He emphasized that it would be a nice tie-in to the book I was writing. My interest was certainly piqued, and my impulse was to accept the offer on the spot. I knew deep down that this was my destiny, but it had to be copacetic with my colleagues at work because of the investment of time involved. I told Jeff that if he could clear it with the publisher of my newspaper, he could count me in.

"Done deal" he said.

I admired his good forward-thinking.

A few days later it was official, and Jeff welcomed me as a 2010 Fight for Charity participant. Training would start on Tuesday, July 6th, two or three times a week plus sparring sessions; he would e-mail me the details. I was excited to be involved and looked forward to getting started, but I hadn't had a fight of any kind in years. How tough was this going to be?

In anticipation of starting the training, I went out to the garage and finally removed the speed bag and heavy bag stand from its box. I assembled it and built a little boxing gym. I know that some decisions in life happen for a reason, and it could take months or even years for the purpose to manifest. The reason for my impulse purchase of that equipment during the holiday season was now obvious.

I contacted a friend of mine named Cindy for some advice and a recommendation on the best trainer and boxing gym. Cindy was part of the group that put together the original Fight for Charity event, so she knew the right people. She suggested Ray Bettinelli and BCBA (Bettinelli's Community Boxing Academy) because she felt that he shared my passion, not only for the sport, but also for my journey. Her advice resonated with me as I recalled my brief interaction with Ray at the last event and felt a connection with him.

I finished setting up my garage with the speed bag, heavy bag, and martial arts Body Opponent Bag that I had purchased many years earlier. I put on the

Rocky soundtrack, and it brought back memories of the day when my brother Sal and I saw the original movie for the very first time.

The one thing I wanted was to get in some practice hitting the speed bag before going to the gym. It was a badge of honor to look like I knew what I was doing. I selected the song "Philadelphia Morning" and slowly started tapping the speed bag. My boxing journey would officially become a mission to universally understand the meaning of the word *success*.

For the next few weeks, I worked out at home in anticipation of the start of training. Coach Ray sent an e-mail listing the things I would need, such as hand wraps and an exercise mat. I had to smile because in the trunk of my car were the hand wraps from my *Rocky* promotion years earlier. I was ready to participate in something I had dreamed about doing and it was all falling into place.

I called Jimmy Gambina to share the news about stepping into the ring and to remark on the coincidence of this connection between us. We discussed my homework assignment to watch the other fight films. Here was another great tie-in; talking to a real-life professional boxing trainer about my turn in the ring.

I sensed his concern for my safety, especially since he knew I was inexperienced and in my mid-Forties. He definitely understood the dangers of the sport. The strange thing was that Jimmy and I had never met each other in person, but it seemed like he knew me very well and was worried about my new adventure. He said that he wanted to know everything I was doing in training so he could help me. I agreed to keep him informed throughout the process. The guy who trained Rocky was actually going to oversee my very own boxing experience!

My story would become more incredible by the minute. I was grateful for the way every connection, big or small, would lead to the continuation and conclusion of my journey. I was certain that it was motivated by the positive signals from the spiritual energy orb.

ROUND FOURTEEN

Training Montage

It was one hundred degrees on July 6th, my first night of training. I hurried home from work to put on some shorts and a sleeveless T-shirt and then headed over to the gym to start the final leg of my journey. I parked my car under the train tracks next to the gym and looked over at the brick building it was located in.

A pair of red boxing gloves hung over the front door. Once inside, I trekked up the stairs to the second floor, and it hit me how similar it all was to Mighty Mick's.

When I walked into the gym, Ray greeted me with the expression, "Whoa!"

He appeared taken aback, either by my large size or my lack of physical conditioning, I wasn't sure which. He clearly realized he had a project on his hands. All I could think of was how hot it was inside. This place was the real deal, almost exactly as I had imagined a boxing gym would be.

I introduced myself to five other charity boxers, and the training began immediately. We started by running up and down the concrete entrance stairs for two minutes with our fists held in front of our chins. George, one of the coaches, called out to help us keep pace. It was not easy, and I was surprised to have gone the full two minutes. This was what it means to be really out of shape, I gasped. There was a long, tough road ahead of me.

After the running, Ray introduced himself and explained some stretching and strength exercises, especially for the legs. He loved to say, "We build boxers from the ground up." He repeated it over and over again as he walked back and forth, correcting our form. There was no turning back now; we would be training for the next five months. As the gym got hotter, I sweated buckets.

The first session lasted a little more than an hour and included a lot of exercise, some instruction, and friendly insults from the Coach. He enjoyed kidding a girl named Kim from an affluent town about how different this must be from the training at her hundred dollar-an-hour kickboxing class. Weeks later, that same girl would become my lone training partner for several months.

After the first few sessions with Ray, I felt a little more comfortable. We still ran the stairs and did stretching exercises, but now we progressed to the boxer's stance and some punch combinations. After our third session, however, I was surprised to receive an e-mail from our boxing coordinator stating that Coach Ray and the BCBA would no longer be involved in training us—no explanation given.

We had the choice of attending either of two gyms that were both farther away and did not offer the convenience of Tuesday and Thursday workout sessions. I had only the weekend to figure out a new plan or be forced to drop out of what I had just started. The other gyms didn't fit my schedule, and I felt a good vibe about this guy. Coach Ray and I were definitely making a connection, and this was the right place for a reason.

Over the weekend, I did some creative thinking and came up with a solution to the dilemma. I would ask one of my clients to sponsor my training program at the BCBA. My client Rob and his partner John owned an office furniture business and we had known each other for years. Rob is a big *Rocky* fan, and we shared a unique connection from the day we met. I knew he would want to be a part of the journey.

First, I called Coach Ray to explain what I was trying to do to stay with his program. I also checked with the event founders to make sure my plan was cleared through them. Coach Ray told me to come to the gym for my next session, and we would work out the details that night. We did just that. The next day I presented Rob and John the opportunity to sponsor my training; they agreed without hesitation.

The *Rocky* connection had come through once again. As it turned out,

Kim also wanted to keep training at the BCBA, and she worked out her own plan. We became a workout team and the only two charity boxers that Coach Ray represented at the event that November.

Days later, the Fight for Charity organizers called a meeting of the boxers at their office to go over what was expected of us during the next few months. At this meeting, we signed the paperwork for our boxing licenses and were sized for our clothing and equipment. We were told that we would learn our opponent's identity in the beginning of November after a series of sparring sessions.

We all looked around the room, checking each other out to see who matched our age and size and wondered which one we'd be paired with. Initially, I was confident to take on anyone, thinking I would be the largest boxer there. However, one guy on my left looked pretty big; I couldn't tell for sure because he was sitting down. When I overheard him say that he had a size fourteen shoe, I was impressed. He might turn out to be my opponent, but it was too early to worry about that. I dismissed the thought and concentrated on training.

Now that the gym situation was under control, the sessions progressed. Coach Ray was building us into boxers from the ground up. It took a few weeks of conditioning before we were allowed to punch anything. When we were properly prepared, he introduced us to what was called twelve-round circuit training. We did twelve, two-minute, boxing-related activities with a thirty second break between each one. He walked us through each activity and instructed us on the proper technique and form. The circuit included exercises, such as doing circles inside the ring by moving side to side around the ropes, or punching individual bags at various speeds and angles.

He had a computer program that he used as the timekeeper. At the start of each round, it would say, "Seconds out." The bell would ring, and after a minute and forty-five seconds, it would say, "Fifteen seconds." Then the bell rang again and it said, "Time." We would rest for thirty seconds, or until we heard "Seconds out" again, before starting our next exercise. After awhile, I lived by the commands of that computerized timekeeper.

One of my most memorable training experiences came when Coach Ray showed me how to hit the speed bag. I had already been practicing for many weeks at home. I inadvertently learned how to do a very advanced one-count routine from watching a demonstration on the Internet. Most boxers punch the speed bag using a three count, which Coach Ray began to teach me. I positioned myself in front of the bag and slowly punched it at the one count without much speed.

"Now that's a one count," he said. "It's more difficult than a three count."

Before he could finish his words, I picked up tremendous speed and started wailing on the bag as he watched in amazement. When he realized what I was up to, he said, "Now you're showing off; that's a one count. Do you know how difficult it is to do a one count?"

I still chuckle whenever I watch that incident. It so happened that I was videotaping some exercises that day so I could e-mail them to Jimmy Gambina for his review and commentary.

Eventually, I felt comfortable with my training routine, but I lagged behind Kim. She had an easier time with both the exercises and the information that Coach Ray asked us to memorize. We were not allowed to spar with him until we passed his oral quiz on different boxing terms and theories. He always made fun of me for not being able to answer correctly.

With Kim's help, I finally made it through the quiz, and we were ready to spar in the ring against the coach. He had been fighting for about forty years, so he was in good shape. When we stepped into the ring, I marveled at how fast he was with the gloves.

During our first sparring session, I was nervous and started out cautiously when the bell rang. Coach told me to throw some jabs on his lid, meaning his forehead, which was protected by headgear. He just stood there as I threw some uncontested shots. We moved around the ring until he made this unique hissing sound. I felt the instant sting of two leather boxing gloves simultaneously striking both sides of my face. I shook my head; I never saw the shots coming. I only heard the noise, followed by the pain. This was for real. That day, I learned there is a science to this great sport of boxing—and for every action, there is a reaction.

We sparred with Coach Ray once a week, and I was always intimidated by that hissing sound he made every time he threw a punch. Whenever I heard it, it was accompanied by a series of sharp blows to the head or body. But I came to realize that I was a super heavyweight, and I could throw a hard punch, too. Occasionally, I caught Ray with a punch that pushed him back.

He would nod his head to say good shot. When I realized I could do that, my confidence slowly began to improve.

During one sparring session, I felt really good and used my size advantage against him. When the bell rang for the first round, I came out strong and threw some aggressive jabs and hooks. As I lunged at him, it was time for the Coach to teach the student a lesson. He lowered himself, took an angle, and threw a brutal body shot between my midsection and liver. I had never been punched like that in all my life. The blow zapped my wind and strength, and I became a virtual punching bag. He pummeled me with multiple shots as I could no longer breathe or defend myself. As the bell sounded to end the second round, I still couldn't catch my breath.

Another coach named Rick, who was working my corner, was convinced I wasn't training hard enough. As the bell rang for the third round, he yelled at Ray to ease up on me, but that was not going to happen. I couldn't raise my arms, and he beat up on me mercilessly. At the end of the round, he even bopped me on top of my head while standing on one leg like a Three Stooges character. I will never forget the embarrassment of that experience. I suffered the aftereffects of that blow to my midsection for at least two weeks. Days later, I still couldn't breathe normally, and mistook the feeling for a respiratory infection or something like that. Lesson learned: Boxing is a painful sport.

As the calendar rolled into September, Coach Ray told Kim and me not to worry, we still had plenty of time and November was months away. By October, we were getting closer to fight night and wondered who our eventual opponent would turn out to be. Kim worked out at two gyms so she could experience different styles of training. She kept telling me about this big guy named Ed at the Fitness Through Boxing gym. He trained with Coach Rob, a professional boxer and fellow *Rocky* fan. She said that Ed was the guy with a size fourteen shoe and he moved around the ring quickly like he was experienced. Kim guessed he would probably be my opponent, and a formidable one, at that.

The opponent-matching sparring sessions began in October. Coach Ray preached safety first, so you knew you wouldn't get hurt too badly with him, but getting into the ring with an unknown was nerve wracking. I tried to verify that Ed was the guy I thought he was, but it was confusing because Kim had gotten his name wrong. The big guy she talked about was Mark O'Loughlin, a local businessman that I knew nothing about. That surprised me since I thought that I knew just about everyone in the local business community. But one thing I did know for sure: He was a big man.

The first real sparring session was scheduled for a Saturday afternoon in October, and I was nervous about the unknown. On the Thursday before, I stopped into Jeff's office to take care of some missing paperwork for my boxing license. I told him about my sparring sessions with Coach Ray and how I still felt the effects of that blow to my midsection. I was uneasy about Saturday's sparring session and wondered who my opponent would be. Jeff tried to reassure me and even suggested we could go a round against each other at the sparring session. He had been boxing and training for more than ten years, and his passion for the sport led him to get involved in this annual charity event. He was not in my weight class, but felt that because of his current lack of training, we would make a good matchup.

We were scheduled to show up at 2 p.m. at Kayo Boxing, another local gym, owned by Coach Michael, a trainer and professional kick boxer. I woke up that morning wondering how the day would turn out. When I arrived at the gym, I heard Coach Michael saying that I was the only heavyweight there, and he wondered who I would match up with. This gym was much different from the BCBA, and as I looked around and saw *Rocky* posters and action figures hanging on the walls, I figured the odds were in my favor.

The girls sparred first, and Kim took advantage of two different opponents. I then watched two middleweights fight a round. I remembered both of them from the early training sessions at the BCBA, but they switched to this gym when Coach Ray dropped out as an official participating training center. I knew that one of them was into martial arts; he was in excellent shape and had some boxing experience. The other was in good condition as well, but I didn't know much about him.

"Hey Big Guy, you're next against this guy," Coach Michael yelled over to me and pointed to the martial arts fighter. I was fresh, and he had just fought a two-minute round.

I was still unsure of myself, even though I was clearly bigger than my opponent. Early in the round, I threw a few ineffective jabs and then felt a hard shot to my jaw that caused something like a blue flash of light in my eyes. I had never experienced anything like that before and recognized again the competitive nature of this sport. I then settled in and took cautious control of the round, even though I was under pressure from the faster opponent.

At one point, Coach Michael yelled to his fighter to go for the body. As he made his move, I hit him with a large right hand to his midsection that knocked him across the ring. He was never the same after that shot, and in the last fifteen seconds of the round, I delivered a combination of eight unanswered blows to his head. He looked stunned at the end and was probably relieved when the bell rang. I was now feeling pretty good about my first real sparring performance.

I was then asked to go against the other smaller opponent. My size advantage was again overwhelming, and I even stopped throwing punches toward the end of the first round. The coach told us to go another one with each other. This time, I just moved around as my opponent covered up his head in defense, throwing a few wild blows. Coach Michael yelled that I was not a punching bag and to throw punches. I forced the other fighter into the corner and pressured him with a series of hooks to the head. One sharp left eventually knocked him down and through the ring ropes. It was my very first knockout ever. I was excited, but concerned for my opponent. I must admit that it felt pretty good, even though I had that unfair advantage.

After my third round of sparring, I thought it was over for the day until I noticed Jeff had his gloves on. He said that maybe we could just go with a one-minute round or two. He told me not to worry, that we'd only work the body.

With that said, I felt comfortable about fighting my fourth round of the day. As the bell rang, Jeff's first punch went directly to the area where Coach Ray had hit me, the same painful spot I had told him about two days earlier. His next blow was not to the body, but an angle shot to my TMJ on the right side of my jaw. I had honestly believed that we were only working the body, but now it was clear: I had just been officially introduced to the sport of boxing.

Jimmy Gambina in one of our telephone conversations had warned me about the dangers of being in the ring. He said that boxing is an unpredictable sport, filled with ego, and cautioned me to protect myself at all times, no matter who my opponent was.

"There are a lot of false promises in this sport," he said.

My jaw throbbed in pain as I began to use a jab tactic called a "slap, tap, and rap" that I learned from Coach Ray. First, my right hand slaps down my opponent's jab. Then I quickly come back and tap him in the grill, meaning his face, followed by a hook to the head. For the next thirty seconds, I slapped, tapped and rapped Jeff multiple times and took full control of the round. When the bell rang, I was still smarting from the blow to my injured midsection, and the muscle in my jaw ached from his well-placed jab. I was furious about the sharp blow because supposedly we were only going to work the body. I learned another important lesson the hard way.

When the bell rang for a second round, I went to work on Jeff and hit him often. Midway through the second one-minute round, he asked to stop because he was winded. In the end, it turned out to be a very good sparring session and a quality learning experience. I now knew, and certainly felt from the pain in my jaw, that my time in the ring was for real.

The following Tuesday, Coach Ray was happy to hear about the results of our first sparring session. I think he especially enjoyed hearing how well the slap, tap, and rap worked for both of us. That night, Kim gave me more information about this big guy named Mark from the other gym. She again mentioned that he had excellent skills. I didn't know if her report was helpful or not, but it sure got my attention. It was mandatory that we attend and participate in three out of four scheduled sparring sessions, so I figured I would run into the man with the size fourteen shoe in the very near future.

Two weeks later, we were scheduled to spar at Body Shots gym for our second session. It took place on a late Saturday afternoon, and I spent the early morning, plus an hour-long car ride, worried about who I would face that day. When I arrived, there were some unfamiliar faces, but once again I was still the biggest guy there.

This gym was run by Coach Eric, who was also a professional boxer. The first thing I noticed was a sign on the wall that said, "Listen to the coach at all times." I wondered if this sparring session was going to be like the last one, with us fighting multiple rounds against numerous opponents. Coach Eric quickly got things started by making each of us go a practice round that consisted of throwing and catching light jabs with a sparring partner. I was told to go into the ring and work with an experienced charity boxer who has fought the last seven years at the event. He, too, was much smaller than me. After the round, this experienced boxer told me about a couple of things that I did wrong and suggested ways to correct my technique. I politely nodded in appreciation and thanked him.

Moments later, I entered the ring to spar with my first heavyweight opponent, a guy named Dan "The Hit Man," who worked for a local business machine company. Dan seemed liked a motivated guy and a quality opponent. I noticed right away that he was a southpaw. I had never fought a lefty before, and knew this would be a much different session. When the bell rang to start the round, he came out strong, coming from the left side with his punches. It easily threw me off. He hit me hard and often, landing two perfect shots to my midsection in that same vulnerable spot. But this time I was prepared, and took both blows easily. As the round continued, I answered his shots with hard ones of my own. I landed consistently with jabs, while again using the slap, tap, and rap technique to my full advantage. In the end, it was a good competitive round, and I even managed to get the advantage. Afterward, I approached Dan to congratulate him and recap the round with him, but he was not very talkative, so I turned and walked away.

In the meantime, Jeff complimented Kim and me on the skills we had learned. He said that we were both standout fighters in the group. Moments later, I was sent back into the ring for another round against the experienced guy who gave me some advice earlier. The round quickly turned into a mismatch. He tried to throw some body blows, but each time I responded with straight, hard rights over the top, striking him in the upper portion of his head. One shot even spun his headgear around over his eyes and caused the round to be stopped. It was the equivalent of a technical knockout, but once again, he was a smaller opponent. Even so, I was feeling good about myself and the whole experience.

At this point, Coach Eric called me over to his corner and instructed me to go back in for another round with Dan the Hit Man. He said to make it a light round, emphasizing the word light, meaning jabs only, and for us to move around the ring together. As I turned away, Coach Eric pulled my arm back and repeated the words, "a light round."

He then shouted over to Dan to make sure he understood the directions also. When the bell rang, we both started throwing jabs, following the coach's instructions, just like the sign on the wall commanded. Toward the end of the round, I began to overuse the old slap, tap, and rap. I connected with about a dozen jabs to the Hit Man's jaw. I got so caught up concentrating on this technique that, with about ten seconds left in the round, Dan hauled off and hit me with all his might, a straight left to my jaw. The blow sent me reeling clear across the ring. I backpedaled several steps on wobbly legs, but stayed on my feet.

I never saw it coming, nor did I expect anyone would throw that kind of punch at a charity sparring session after being instructed to go "a light round." It was a questionable shot that absolutely found its mark and did its damage. I got my bell rung and never had a chance to answer back, since it came at the very end of the round. I immediately turned to Coach Eric, and in not-so-kind words, demanded an explanation of what had just happened.

He looked at me, shrugged and said, "Two things: One you should always keep your hands up, and two, never trust anybody in the ring."

I was perplexed, and had no reply. It was the most valid boxing advice I'd ever been given. Days later, I was still feeling the effects of that blow.

The following Tuesday night, I skipped my regular in-gym sparring session to get some much needed rest. Later that week, Coach Ray, Kim and I talked about how some of the sparring sessions placed visiting boxers at a disadvantage; we had to be cautious for the next one.

By this time, the calendar had changed to November, and we were three weeks away from the big night. On the first Monday of the month, we would finally learn who our actual opponents were going to be at a pre-party to promote the event. In talking it over with Coach Ray and Kim, we agreed that I would either get a return match with Dan the Hit Man or it would be Mark O'Loughlin, the guy that Kim spoke so highly about. Her comments even piqued Coach Ray's interest to find out a little more about him. By this point, I had grown closer to Coach Ray, and we talked about my journey many times. He knew what motivated me to be part of this event, and as my coach or manager, he also wanted to protect me.

At the networking party, I learned that my opponent would be big Mark. The organizers picked the largest guy in the room to go up against me. I also learned some additional information about him. He was a building manager for a commercial property management company. He was three inches taller than me, thirty pounds heavier, ten years younger, and had a six-inch reach advantage. He also was the father of three young children.

In my mind, this information provided a small sense of relief that this giant wasn't out to totally destroy me. It would probably be a good, clean fight. Being a father of three also explained his fighting nickname, "Fatty Daddy." My moniker was "Best of LI," after that awards program I ran for the *Long*

Island Press, but standing next to this Goliath, I was feeling nothing like the best. To make matters worse, someone mentioned that Mark had previous experience fighting in the Golden Gloves. Coach Ray was now seriously concerned for my well-being, and I could not believe that I was going to be, of all things, an underdog in a boxing match. The final irony of my *Rocky* story had become reality.

My third sparring session was set for the next Saturday, and I was expected to go three two-minute rounds with Mark. During training that week, Coach Ray turned the excitement of my journey into a real concern. He talked about Mark's size advantage and his experience in the ring. Kim continued to speak of his speed. I was now seriously concerned, especially coming off my latest injury from the recent blow to my head. I was no longer confident about this whole boxing experience—these punches were real, and they were adding up.

Coach Ray made sure that both he and Coach George from our gym joined me at the sparring session at Mark's home gym. He was concerned about my opponent, in view of what happened at the last gym, and he wanted to be there to support me.

Earlier in the week, I had received some photographs taken at the networking event that showed a pre-fight photo of Mark and me with our clenched fists up against each other. I'm a big man, but this guy's fists, arms, and reach seemed to be twice the size of mine. He looked invincible, and his reputation as the "Big Guy" was quickly growing. All week long, my coworkers who saw the picture would laugh and say I didn't have a prayer against the big guy. I became more and more anxious every time someone called me crazy for getting into the ring with him.

Saturday afternoon, I arrived at the gym and was happy to see both Coach Ray and George there to support me, along with one of their heavyweight students. As we got ready for the day's sparring session, I spoke with Mark and learned a little more about him. He was, indeed, not only an experienced boxer, but a football player, a football coach, marathon runner, and triathlete. I was impressed and respected why this event was important to him. The interesting thing was that he once weighed over three hundred pounds, and worked hard to get back into shape. This boxing event was a catalyst for achieving one of his personal goals; he currently weighed in around two hundred eighty pounds. While he was an awfully big man, I learned that he was also a gentleman. I knew that my hands were full, but I felt certain he would box under control and be responsible, although you never know for sure once the bell rings.

There was no time to procrastinate, as Mark and I were selected to go first and fight our three, two-minute rounds. All I could think about was protecting my face from savage blows like the one I received at the last sparring session. I took a slow, timid approach to the bout, throwing some effective jabs. Suddenly, Mark landed a thunderous jab to my mouth, which immediately fattened and bruised my lip. That was the hardest I'd been hit throughout the whole experience. After being hit hard on every shot, I managed to survive the first round, trying desperately to protect my face. Both Coach Ray and Jeff were concerned about the shot to my mouth. As they checked my bruised and swelling lip, they had me worried, too.

In the second round, I took a few more power shots to the face, with one bruising my nose. I tried to slow him down, but Mark was tough to hold off. The third round turned a little sloppy as we both seemed to tire, but I felt it was my best round. I was pleased to have survived with only minimal damage, and even though my nose and lip were hurting, I was feeling upbeat about my performance.

Later, Coach Michael wanted to send me back into the ring to fight a round with one of his heavyweights, a lawyer named Rich, whose opponent was to be Dan the Hit Man. When Coach Michael gestured for me to enter the ring, Coach Ray jumped up and denied his request.

"My fighter's done for the day. He went his three rounds already."

I was glad I didn't have to face yet another opponent, but then Mark volunteered to go another round with the lawyer. Now I felt stupid because he had already gone three with me and was still willing to go one more, like it was nothing. But I was relieved to be done sparring for the day, and this would give me an opportunity to observe Mark in action. I wasn't sure that Rich was comfortable fighting a round with the big man.

As they bounced around getting ready, I settled in to watch up close. When the bell rang, Rich charged out of his corner like a wild person, swinging at Mark with reckless abandon. I was surprised by his approach toward the larger man. Then, it happened as if in slow motion. Mark took one step back, and with the same ferocious jab that had fattened my lip, he cut loose and broke this poor guy's nose. That one shot gave notice to all that

Mark was for real, and it confirmed to me that I was going up against one hellacious fighter.

I suspected that maybe Mark had been holding back against me during our sparring session, and come fight night I would be in real trouble. These worries crept into my psyche and festered there. I left the gym a little sore, but happy that it seemed to go well. There had been no cheap shots like those in the last two sessions, and my bruised lip made me look sort of like a tough guy. One thing was clear, however: I was definitely the underdog.

That night, I took my family out to dinner to relax and forget about all of this boxing stuff that was running through my mind. We were having a pleasant evening until I received a text message from Coach Ray.

"We have some work to do. You did well today, but you got beat, and lost all three rounds. We need to talk on Tuesday."

I texted back my impression that I did better than he thought. Coach Ray countered that as an experienced boxing coach, he knew best. My happy mood turned to apprehension. I didn't stand a chance against the big guy.

Back at the office on Monday morning, Jed asked how the sparring session went on Saturday. I explained that my opponent was formidable—huge and highly experienced. I was a dead man. How ironic that I was the underdog, just like Rocky Balboa.

"I don't think I can win," I told Jed. "I just want to go the distance."

He smiled and shook his head; he knows me well and already read a draft version of this book, so he was familiar with my journey. It was clearly time for me to go to work and prepare my body, mind and spirit for the upcoming battle.

Back at the gym on Tuesday night, Coach Ray went on and on about how I didn't stand a chance.

"This guy's a ringer," he warned. "Did you see what he did to that other guy's nose? You shouldn't be in there with him."

But that wasn't an option, I suggested that we build a strategy to go against the more experienced fighter. Maybe I should learn more about blocking in order to take fewer power shots to the head. Ray agreed, but remained extremely concerned about my chances. This really ramped up my nervousness. I reminded him about the irony of being the underdog and how it related to my journey. We just smiled at each other.

Since I had already attended my three mandatory sparring sessions, I decided to skip the last one. We were way too close to the event to chance another uncontrolled encounter. Instead I chose to spar with Coach Ray's other heavyweight student, another guy named Mark, who was twenty years younger than me and aiming to turn professional.

This Mark not only hit with stinging power, but he was fast and shifted quickly about the ring. I was no match for him, but I used the experience to learn how to block punches and chase the faster man. My confidence had sunk to its lowest level ever. What was I doing in the boxing ring, especially at my age?

That night I reached out to Jimmy Gambina for some extra advice, and we had an hour-long conversation about the challenge ahead of me. He preached the importance of working the body at a lower angle to take advantage of the taller man.

The next day, Jeff called to find out why I wasn't at the sparring session and to let me know there'd been a change of plans. Since Rich the lawyer broke his nose, his opponent, Dan the Hit Man, would now fight my opponent Mark. I was paired against some new guy named Joe who wasn't currently training, but had experience fighting in past events. Jeff gave me the option to fight Rich if I wanted to, but I would have to hold back from hitting him in the face. I was confused by these choices and not sure what to do.

My first reaction was relief that I didn't have to go up against the big guy. After all, everyone said I didn't have a chance against him. On the one hand, I was glad but lurking in the back of my mind was the knowledge that this was taking the easy way out. It contradicted everything the Rocky Spirit stands for. If I had learned one thing on this journey, it was to face my challenges head-on. This new guy, Joe, was an unknown entity. At least Mark was enough of a gentleman, that if he was killing me, he would probably pull back a little. I figured Coach Ray would know what was best for me, and suggested that Jeff talk to him for a decision.

Ray called the next day to inform me that I had a new opponent. He knew Joe and said this was a better match-up because of my lack of ring experience. We would discuss it on Tuesday. When he hung up the telephone, I had the feeling that I had just cheated myself. I was destined to be the underdog at this event. It didn't really matter if I won or not, as long as I went the distance without getting hurt.

When I arrived at the gym Tuesday night, I learned that things had changed once again. I was back against Mark because Dan the Hit Man didn't want any part of the big guy. That clinched it: I was going to get killed in there. The only thing I could do now was to work on my game plan and prepare myself for the fight.

Jeff joined us for a training session that night, and I sparred with Coach Ray one last time. I landed a few good shots, which boosted my confidence. I also thought I might have avenged that humiliating "Three Stooges" punch to the head he had given me weeks earlier. Later that night, I regained some self-assurance when Jeff commented on a Facebook post that he had watched me spar at the gym, and I was definitely ready.

The big fight was now little more than a week away, and I was consumed by everything related to this entire experience. The next Tuesday at the gym, I met Joe for the first time and sparred three awkward, but controlled rounds with him. Afterward, Joe told us about his recent sparring session against Dan the Hit Man. He didn't like how the aggressive guy handled himself, especially since Joe hadn't trained at all for this event. He said he felt more comfortable facing me. Coach Ray was now convinced that I should fight Joe. He was going to contact Jeff to make the change and would call me later.

It sounded like my coach had lost confidence in me, but in reality, as an experienced boxing man, he was just trying to protect me. Coach Ray called later to say that Jeff would have to talk to the other fighters before he could make the change.

By Friday of that week, I still hadn't heard back from anyone about the switch. Three days before the big fight, all the charity boxers were to be at the Fitness Through Boxing gym at five in the morning to promote the event on the local morning news program. I arrived a little behind schedule, and the first person I ran into was Mark. He put me on the spot by asking why I didn't want to fight him. I said it was my coach's decision, and I wasn't looking to get busted up. Mark agreed that the night wasn't about that. He thought it would be a good competitive match, and he hoped I'd change my mind.

After we taped the news segment, which got me some good camera time, Jeff approached me to ask what the deal was. I claimed to be all right with boxing Mark and told him that Coach Ray was making me crazy by saying I didn't stand a chance. Jeff said he had seen me spar, and I did have a chance. He decided that everything would stay the same, and I would once again officially be on with Mark. The roller coaster ride of emotions never seemed to end, but the journey was back on track and I began to truly get focused.

I had a few last-minute details to take care of over the final weekend. One of them was to receive an old-style blessing. I planned on attending mass on Sunday morning at our local church Maria Regina with my daughters. We would first pray to St. Anthony to protect me and my opponent. I requested that we have a spirited match and neither of us would sustain an injury. I prayed to my father and an old friend, Michael Mullan, to safeguard me in battle. Mullan was a fireman who perished years earlier at the World Trade Center on September 11, 2001. I figured it could only help to have all of the good spirits in my corner.

After the silent prayer, I needed an old-fashioned Father Carmine-type blessing by one of the priests. I walked to the exit at the back of the church and explained to Father Allan why I was requesting this blessing. He smiled in agreement. As I bowed my head, he raised both hands over me and prayed to Jesus for my safety and the fulfillment of my journey. As he performed the blessing, a warm sensation came over me, like a large cloak of protection. It was an incredible feeling and an amazing connection to the Lord. After the blessing, I knew that I was spiritually prepared to finish my journey.

Later that night at around 8 p.m., I received an e-mail from the charity saying I could stop by the hotel to pick up my boxing gear. I wasted no time getting over there and hoped to get a look at the ballroom and the ring, if possible.

The first thing I did at the hotel was to look into the room where the boxing ring would be the next night, where I would finally stand before a large audience. For a moment, I visualized myself being successful in that very room. Then I turned around to look for the equipment. When I couldn't find anyone, I sent an e-mail to the girl from the charity to ask for directions. They had not left for the hotel yet so I headed down the road to pick up my equipment at their office. That's where I saw the lineup card and confirmed that our contest would be the eleventh of twelve fights. It was going to be a long night.

Back home, I tried on the clothing so my girls could see me all dressed up, and we took some photographs. Then I packed my bag with everything I would need for the next day. The only thing left was to call Jimmy Gambina for any final strategic advice.

Jimmy once again stressed the importance of going to the body on different levels when fighting a taller man. This included lowering my body to land more leveraged punches. For over half an hour I listened closely to every piece of advice. But it was getting late, and I needed plenty of sleep. I thanked him for all of his help and support over the last few months. Before I hung up the telephone, Jimmy asked if he could pray for me. When I enthusiastically agreed, he offered another prayer to Jesus for my safety and guidance as I finish my lifelong journey. His amazing prayer lasted for seven minutes. It was incredible how I made a connection to this man that I had never even met in person. When I hung up the telephone, there was no doubt in my mind that I was ready for this next chapter; it was my destiny to perform. Gambina's prayer was exceptional and motivating—he completely understood every aspect of my journey as if he had known me forever.

Throughout my training experience, I recognized the importance of maintaining confidence and a positive thought process. By allowing a negative thought into my head it had a chance to grow wild like a weed. I knew what was needed and used visualization and meditation to get focused. It also helped to be spiritually supported and I thought about the orb as I packed the photograph in my gym bag along with the one of Dad. I was about to turn the page toward the final round of my journey.

ROUND FIFTEEN

Fight Night

It was November 22, 2010 and the big day finally arrived. I was ready to step into a boxing ring—there was no turning back. The minute my eyes opened that morning, nervous excitement flooded over, around, and through me. I rehearsed my role in the evening's events over and over in my head. By that time, I knew exactly how I would enter the ring, at what pace I would take the fight, and how I would tackle the first round. I even saw how I would finish, including my actions once it was over. I visualized it all in my mind and was fully prepared.

The morning began like any other. I left for work early to attend a few meetings, my goal was to return home by 2:30, to gather what was needed, make some last-minute ticket arrangements, and reach the hotel by 4 o'clock. The day went smoothly and I arrived at home as planned and readied myself for the big night.

I got into my car at 3:30 and punched up a special CD, disc four, track five, on my ten-disc changer: "War/Fanfare" from *Rocky*. I was on my way to the hotel, full of confidence.

When I arrived, the energy level was already in motion, and most of the setup was complete. I entered the main room to familiarize myself with the ring, which was now in place and would be the center of all of the action. As I gazed at the squared circle, I reflected on five long months of training, sparring sessions, massive blows to the head, and my lifelong journey coming to a conclusion. I took a deep breath and walked out to look for the dressing room. We were scheduled to weigh in at 4:30 with a boxer meeting at 5 p.m.

When I located the dressing room, I discovered it was not private. People were coming in and out, and we were all jumbled together. I greeted everyone and looked around for my opponent, but he wasn't there yet. After getting dressed, I headed over to the weigh-in for my prefight medical checkup from the ringside doctor. I handed in my yellow passbook to a member of the boxing association in charge of the event. This was my boxing license, and it would be used to log in the official results of the bout. At the end of a fight in a charity exposition such as this, the referee raises the hand of both fighters in victory in front of the crowd, but the real sanctioned judges actually log the win or loss scoring results into your passbook.

I stepped on the scale and weighed in, having dropped ten pounds. That was a good weight loss, and I had also added muscle, especially in my upper torso. Even my face showed that I was thinner. After the weigh in, the doctor took my blood pressure, checked my breathing, and asked some questions: Did I have any recent injuries or surgeries? Was I currently taking any medication? I replied no and was finished with my pre-fight check up.

I turned around and finally saw my opponent wearing red shorts, a red tank top, and black shoes; he reminded me of the character Ivan Drago in *Rocky IV*. I was dressed in all blue with *Long Island Press* written across the back of my tank top and Little Vincent's Pizza, a popular eatery and a sponsor, written on the front of my shorts. I greeted Mark and when we shook hands, he asked if I was ready.

"As long as you take it easy on me."

I joked about his size, remarking that he looked even bigger in his shorts and tank top. He told me not to worry, that we would have a good, clean fight. As I mentioned before, this was a milestone for Mark on his personal journey of weight loss and getting back into fighting shape. This challenge was important to him, too. The spirit of his success was to get back in that ring and compete. Even though I was only a few hours away from throwing punches with this guy, I found it hard not to like him. He was a good man and something connected our journeys.

For the next four hours, we would be together in and out of the dressing room, anticipating our turn. Coach Ray wrapped my hands early so the head referee could initial them proving that it was inspected and done properly.

One of Ray's assistant coaches, a guy named Al, asked if I had seen the special headgear that Coach had chosen for me to wear that night. I hadn't. Coach Ray smiled and pulled out a red, white, and blue American flag headgear. It was his own personal equipment that he had worn in big fights. He placed it on my head to size me.

"Here you go, Rock, I brought this especially for you."

It was an unexpected Rocky touch and an honor to be wearing Coach Ray's colors. I beamed in gratitude and thanked him for his kind gesture. He completely understood this journey.

After getting my hands wrapped, I took a walk to see what was going on outside and in the main arena. I wanted to see if all of my guests had arrived. Every time I checked, someone would ask me who I was fighting. When I pointed to big Mark, they always laughed.

"Good luck, Felice, you're going to need it. Did you see the size of that guy?"

Such comments chipped away at my confidence. Of course I knew it wasn't going to be easy, but I was still ready. I greeted most of my guests, which included my wife Chrissy, family members, coworkers, business associates and friends. They gave me good support that night.

I then returned to the dressing room to sit and wait my turn. Part of my strategy was to not waste any energy. In my pre-fight plan, I considered an odd lesson that I learned while watching the *Rocky Balboa* movie. When Rocky adopted a dog, he chose the one that was lying still and not expending its energy. He said the dog was smart. I personally had seen too many athletes in my sports life get all hyped before an event and then fall flat. I was not going to let that happen to me; I had a perfect vision of what I needed to do. I would walk slowly into the ring and stand still. There would be no bouncing around or throwing air punches. I wouldn't waste any energy; it would all be focused in my mind and heart. I would just concentrate on the final result of my journey and the success of going the distance to experience the actual feeling of the Rocky Spirit.

I only left the dressing room to handle any ticket situations and watch my training partner fight. I wasn't worried about Kim because in sparring she was highly motivated and had the advantage over her opponent. Her challenger was a late volunteer, and while she was a very nice person, she lacked Kim's skills. In the end, Kim easily won.

The long wait for the eleventh bout of the night was getting to me. One by one, the other fighters returned to the dressing room, either elated over their win or down from their loss or underwhelming experience in the ring. Two of the fighters suffered injuries. As I continued to watch each fighter return, my anxiety spiraled.

Around the end of the seventh fight, my opponent started warming up in front of me with his trainer, throwing some hard blows into the punch mitts. The loud sound from the force of each connection caught my attention. I kept repeating a mantra to myself: Don't get injured and go the distance. It sounds corny, but that's what I wanted to accomplish. My most important goals were to fight a good fight and not sustain any injuries, standing eight counts, and definitely no knockdowns.

Coach Ray noticed that I was paying too much attention to my opponent and suggested that we go into another room for our warm-up. I gloved-up and followed him across the hall. We started moving around, working the punch mitts three minutes at a time. The three rounds that I would fight for this charity event were one minute long, so the three consecutive minutes of punch mitts proved that I had the stamina. However, I did feel a bit stiff after sitting all night.

During the five months of training, one of the things I did not excel in was the punch mitts. I hit hard, but would mess up the count or use the wrong hand. That night as I was warming up, Coach Ray called for a one, meaning a left-hand jab to his mitt, but I threw a two, a straight right. He dropped his hands in frustration.

"Are you kidding me? Five months of training and you can't get this right?" he shouted. "Come on now, concentrate."

I shook my head and continued my warm-up. When we stopped, they were up to the ninth fight. My moment of truth was right around the corner. The fight coordinator called for us to get ready and put our robes on. Coach Ray and his team, Coach Duke and Al, helped me with my robe. On the back of this shiny blue garment there was no "Italian Stallion" or Shamrock Meats. It said Felice "Best of LI" Cantatore. This was my time to be the best, to do more than go the distance.

Both teams of trainers led their fighters into the hallway and over to the kitchen doors. We were supposed to walk through the kitchen corridor and wait by the entrance of the ballroom to watch the entire fight before us. I followed behind my opponent, intimidated by his large frame. He stopped at the first set of doors, and I continued on to the second. There I met up with my brother Sal and coworker Harlan, who were part of the entourage that would escort me into the ring. When the two fighters ahead of me made their entrance, the house deejay played the *Rocky* theme song. I felt relieved because I didn't want the added pressure of entering the ring to that music myself. I had mentioned it earlier to a few people, including my sister Doreen, who was standing nearby, about to explode with excitement over this fight. She looked ready to go into the ring for me.

While waiting in the doorway, I started to lose focus. I could see my brother watching my every move as I did another quick warm-up on the punch mitts. Harlan stood there talking about how cool the whole experience was. Coach Al kept trying to build up my confidence by telling me that I was ready. Sal, Harlan and I were all in a place we had never been before. The ultimate challenge confronted us, man-on-man in the middle of a boxing ring. It was time. Were we ready?

Coach Ray turned to me and got nose-to-nose. He looked into my eyes and addressed me in a quiet, but motivating, voice. As our energies connected, he said:

> "This is it, the moment you've been waiting for since you were a kid and watched Rocky for the very first time. It's the moment you trained over five months for, the moment that you wrote a book about and are waiting to finish. This is your moment, Felice. You created it and manifested it as an eleven-year-old boy. Tonight you will write the final chapter of your book. You already know the ending; you wrote it in your vision. Now go out there and finish your journey."

In an unexplainable flash of clarity, Coach Ray Bettinelli's words turned everything around. There were no more butterflies or nerves, just undivided focus. It was as if Coach Ray had transferred a super burst of energy directly into my very spirit and soul that was already protected by prayer.

At that precise time, the kitchen doors swung wide open to the stirring music of "Eye of the Tiger," blaring from the house speakers. Doreen secretly asked the deejay to play that song when my turn came to enter the ring. It was the perfect selection and motivated me to the highest level of vibrational energy. This truly was my moment and destiny; I possessed the Eye of the Tiger.

I slowly entered the arena with my black gloves resting on Coach Ray's shoulders, followed by my entourage: Coaches Duke and Al, Sal, and Harlan, just as I had envisioned it. Again, I didn't waste any energy. There was no bouncing around, only a deliberate, measured walk to the ring.

Coach Ray held the ropes open for me to climb through. Once inside, I stood still in my corner and watched my much larger opponent bounce up and down to ready himself. In slow motion, my eyes observed a large man dressed all in red with lots of hair sticking out from his tank top. I focused on his black mouthpiece. "The Eye of the Tiger" continued to blast in the background as the crowd cheered, chanting both Rocky and Felice. I was zoned in like never before. Tinseltown may have been thousands of miles away, but this was a Hollywood movie, and I was the star, it was my *Rocky*.

I faced my corner to make the sign of the cross and punch the turnbuckle for good luck. Coach Ray had instructed me to never turn my back on an opponent, so I turned around and stood still as I waited for the introductions.

"Folks, this going to be a great heavyweight fight," the announcer said. "In the red corner is Mark "Fatty Daddy" O'Loughlin, and in the blue corner, we have Felice "Best of LI" Cantatore."

The referee came over to check my gloves and told me to follow his commands at all times. The next five minutes would be a microcosm of my journey that began in a candy store as an eleven-year-old boy, until now as I stood in a boxing ring, a forty-five year-old man.

Just seconds later, the bell rang, and in my mind, everything went silent. I didn't even hear the screaming crowd. I slowly moved to the center of the ring and threw the first jab of the contest, connecting to the jaw of my looming opponent. He jabbed back, and I blocked it, countering with another one of my own and surprisingly connecting again. As he threw another jab and a straight right-hand, I crouched down, took an angle and delivered a few hooks to the body. Bam—just like I had imagined it the night before, and just like Jimmy had counseled. I landed the blows and scored on each one. I managed to avoid some of his punches, as if I were being protected by a mysterious force of energy. The first round went quickly, and when I returned to my corner and sat on the stool, Coach Ray said:

"You won that round. You did great. Now keep going to the body, land your jabs where I showed you and keep your hands up."

Hearing Coach Ray say that I won the first round was motivating, especially after all the times he told me that I got killed in the sparring session.

The bell rang for Round Two, and this time Mark came out swinging. Clearly, the second round was not going to be easy. I backed off and kept my distance most of the time as he banged away. I tied him up a few times and continued to score with the jab. Suddenly, I took a crashing right-cross to the head and saw the ominous flash of blue light that follows a well-connected blow. For the very first time, I heard the crowd gasp at the sound of the punch. It was a massive shot, and just like that, I was in trouble. I took a step back to get my bearings and kept my hands up to protect myself. He threw another walloping right-hand that didn't connect as well, but it drew enthusiastic applause from the crowd. I managed to tie him up again and did enough to score some additional points of my own. Seconds later, the bell sounded to end the round.

As I headed back to my corner, Coach Ray refocused me on my mission and told me that Mark was tired. I glanced over, but didn't see what he was seeing. Coach Ray said I had only one more minute to go. I was winning the fight; all that I needed was to finish strong. With that one smashing blow to the head, I didn't feel like I was winning anything. Everything was happening so fast. One more round injury-free and I will have gone the distance.

Mark came out strong again in the Third Round as I threw jabs and hooks to the body, connecting numerous times. The left-to-liver was my best punch; it slowed him down as we went toe to toe. We were both competing at the highest level with a goal of finishing strong. I ended the round by throwing a multiple-punch combination. As the final bell rang, we clutched in a hug of appreciation in the center of the ring, exactly as I had imagined it. I then turned to face the side of the ring where Chrissy, my family, and friends were standing, and I raised my arms Rocky-style, straight up to the heavens. Those who knew about my quest understood the meaning of my gesture. It wasn't about boxing; it represented an everyman's journey in life, and a connection to personal success.

As for the results, it didn't really matter how it turned out; the important thing was that I did it. It was all about the Rocky Spirit—that carried me to this ultimate moment. The referee called both of us to the center of the ring and raised our arms as they did with all of the charity fighters. I was sky-high excited as he presented me with a trophy and handed back my yellow passbook. I noticed the look of appreciation for my efforts on Coach Ray's face. My success was his success; the positive energy was spreading across the entire room.

As I left the ring, I was greeted by everyone who came out to support me. We were exuberant over what had just taken place. I gave Chrissy a celebratory hug and kiss. Throughout the night she filmed all the excitement on her cell phone. Then I found Jed and lifted him clear off the ground. We both understood what had just transpired, and we celebrated the journey.

After taking pictures with everyone, it dawned on me to check my yellow book for the official results. I knew I had fought a fight that was well beyond my ability. It just happened that everything I did that night came together and was perfect. With one hand grasping my trophy, I thumbed through the pages of my passbook and found the check-off box—I won by a point's decision.

"I did it! I won the fight!" I was overcome by surprise and sheer happiness. I had lived my spiritual dream with a bona fide Hollywood ending. Coach Ray was right: I had written this ending many years ago, and was destined to live it. That night, all of the positive energy connected to the orb proved to be in my corner.

I ran back through the kitchen corridor toward the dressing room, leaping in the air with my arms raised high. In a frozen second in time, my journey was officially complete. Everything that I ever imagined had come to fruition. Against all odds, I appeared in a *Rocky* movie, attended the gala premiere, became friends with cast members, stepped into the boxing ring as an underdog, emerged a winner and understood the unique connection to spiritual energy confirming that we are all being watched over.

At the same time, I realized that my opponent that night also emerged a winner. Mark chased his own vision to return to the ring and compete on a spirited level. I sensed a link to his story through a lesson learned in the original *Rocky* about the importance of determination and going the distance, no matter the outcome. I appreciated our experience we shared in the boxing ring that night.

Fight Night | 171

Back in the kitchen corridor, just like the ending of a movie, my image slowly faded away. I remained suspended in air with my arms raised to the heavens. It was now clear, the question of who or what guided me to this point was answered at the beginning of the original *Rocky*. The very first seconds of the opening scene in that old church took me full circle to find the answer. This amazing journey proved that an everyman can go the distance to succeed by tapping into personal faith, a passionate heart, and a life's purpose, all of what is considered to be the *Rocky Spirit*.

THE EPILOGUE

Final Bell

Inspiration: A divine influence or action on a person believed to qualify him or her to receive and communicate sacred revelation.

"You already know the ending; you wrote it in your vision. Now go out there and finish your journey."

Moments before entering the ring, those words from my boxing coach resonated through me. All along from the time I was eleven years old to the moment I raised my hands at the end of the last round, there was a spirited connection motivating my destiny. I knew that behind every success is the inspiration that leads to a journey. I also understood that it was a divine influence and a sacred revelation that linked me to the franchise of *Rocky*.

My favorite movies and its main character taught me to never give up and work hard to motivate my body, mind and spirit. To be standing at that final bell no matter the outcome symbolized a willingness to take a chance to succeed. Just like the southpaw from Philly, your passions, heart and soul can help you become "A Somebody." Always believe in yourself and be inspired to accomplish anything that you dare to dream, whether you are reaching for your goals or overcoming obstacles that may be present in your life.

A photograph of a universal energy orb awakened the spiritual awareness within me. This combination communicated that it doesn't matter whether you win or lose or hit a bump in the road, unwavering faith will provide the courage, confidence and wisdom to go the distance. The cast of the original film claimed that God was working in their corner when they created a movie that would influence millions of lives worldwide. It was more than a boxing movie and love story; it was a film about universal and spiritual connections. I am thankful to Sylvester Stallone for introducing Rocky Balboa to the world. His energy gave life to the Italian Stallion. No matter how he got there, he did it—may the spirit of Rocky always be a part of us.

I trust my story will inspire you to achieve your personal goals. It would be an honor to do something significant for others, the way Mr. and Mrs. Gardner, the owners of that luncheonette, did for me when I was a child. Their enthusiastic recommendation had such a powerful effect on my life. It is my intention to do the same for others.

This journey was made possible by the support of my entire family, friends, coworkers, and every person mentioned in this book. I will always cherish the love and joy given to me by my daughters, Gina Marie and Adriana. I treasure my wonderful wife, Chrissy, for her love, faithful support, and patience. Our experience that December night in 2006 at the top of the Rocky Steps produced a magical moment that transcended time.

Look closely at the energy orb in the image on the next page. It is the actual photograph taken by my wife at the end of that incredible evening. It shines bright with a significant meaning. The orb radiating from my energized fist represents a manifestation of *so* many souls. The powerful sign is a confirmation that a spiritual presence is always watching over us, guiding our destiny and desires. It is my prayer that this true story and the energy from the photograph encourage you to attract personal success through your own inspiration, determination and positive thoughts. When you reach the top step of your journey remember to raise your arms straight to the heavens and shout, "Yo, Adrian, I did it!"

To be continued…

Final Bell | 175

To view this photograph and others in full color, please visit www.rockyspirit.org

Anything is possible … with a puncher's chance.
—Felice Cantatore
Rocky Spirit

Made in the USA
San Bernardino, CA
06 November 2013